Wounded Knee 1973

Wounded Knee 1973

A PERSONAL ACCOUNT BY Stanley David Lyman

EDITED BY Floyd A. O'Neil, June K. Lyman, & Susan McKay

FOREWORD BY Alvin M. Josephy, Jr.

University of Nebraska Press / LINCOLN & LONDON

Copyright © 1991 by the University of Nebraska Press
All rights reserved
Manufactured in the United States of America
The paper in this book meets the minimum requirements of American
National Standard for Information Sciences—Permanence of Paper for
Printed Library Materials, ANSI Z39.48–1984.

Library of Congress Cataloging-in-Publication Data
Lyman, Stanley David, 1913–1979.
Wounded Knee 1973: a personal account / Stanley David Lyman;
edited by Floyd A. O'Neil, June K. Lyman, and Susan McKay; foreword
by Alvin M. Josephy, Jr.
p.   cm.
Includes index.
ISBN 0-8032-2889-9 (alk. paper)
1. Wounded Knee (S.D.)—History—Indian occupation, 1973—Personal
narratives.   2. Lyman, Stanley David, 1913–1979—Diaries.   3. United
States.   Bureau of Indian Affairs—Officials and employees—Diaries.
I. O'Neil, Floyd A. (1927?)   II. Lyman, June K., 1912–   .   III. McKay,
Susan, 1948–   .   IV. Title.
E99.03.L96   1991
978.3'66–dc20
                                                    90-12653
                                                    CIP

Contents

Illustrations

Foreword

By Alvin M. Josephy, Jr.

Much has been published about Wounded Knee II, the dramatic seventy-one-day armed siege at the historic hamlet on the Pine Ridge Indian Reservation in South Dakota in the spring of 1973. Most of what has appeared in print, however, has presented the goals, actions, and points of view of the besieged—a determined group of American Indian Movement (AIM) leaders and members, a desperate and angry element of the Pine Ridge Oglala Lakota population, Indians from other reservations and various urban centers, and some non-Indian supporters from different parts of the country. This book tells, with gripping immediacy, what went on among the besiegers.

The episode, deeply rooted in the tortuous history of federal-Indian relations, was the explosive climax of a series of attempts by American Indians, led frequently by the militant leadership of AIM, to attract the attention of the general American population, an indifferent United States government, and the whole world to the continued frustrations and injustices of their daily lives. Their grievances were many and varied, ranging from grinding poverty, ill health, and substandard housing on reservations to the ignoring of treaty rights, the robbing of Indian-owned natural resources, lack of protection from discrimination and prejudice, Bureau of Indian Affairs (BIA) corruption and neglect, and the denial of self-determination and the right to govern themselves and manage and control their own affairs.

In the atmosphere of the "rights revolution" and the new interest in minorities within the United States in the 1960s and early 1970s, the time was ripe for an Indian outburst. At Pine Ridge and other reservations, dissatisfaction became focused on what many Indians perceived to be the root of their problems: a form of tribal government, imposed on them by the United States government in the 1930s, that—to a greater or lesser extent—fastened on them a tribal political leadership whose dependency on federal-government approval in all important matters made them more responsive and responsible to the Bureau of Indian Affairs than to the needs and desires of their own people.

By 1973, on some reservations, including Pine Ridge—as the situation emerges clearly in this book—subtle changes had begun to take place at the reservation level. Under BIA commissioner Louis Bruce, more power and responsibilities were being given to the tribal governments, and the BIA apparatus was being transformed from the role of boss to that of servant of the Indian tribes and their people. Instead of telling the tribal government what to do, the BIA and its personnel would now ask the tribal government what they could do to help and support it. In practice, however, the changes so far had been superficial and largely unrecognized by the reservation populations. The BIA still held the power to approve or veto any important step proposed by the tribal government. Some BIA area directors and reservation superintendents, opposed to losing their authority, resisted giving it up and openly sabotaged Bruce's aims. Finally, during the year prior to the Wounded Knee confrontation, Congress and the secretary of the interior pulled in Bruce's reins, giving support to the resisting BIA personnel and confusing those who, like our author, were striving genuinely to accommodate to a new relationship and now had to wonder about the parameters of their authority and responsibilities. Moreover, the retreat added fuel to the already-blazing anger of freedom-seeking Indians and further fixed in their minds the image of colluding enemies, including the perceived, close-at-hand agents of their oppression and continued dependency, the tribal political leaders and their partners, the local and area BIA officials.

Thus, the clash at Wounded Knee was essentially an Indian "revolution" against the form of government at the Pine Ridge Reservation—a government that was regarded as responsible for the people's grievances—and also against those who personified that government—the tribal chairman, Richard ("Dick") Wilson, and his followers, who were accused of being corrupt and tyrannical, and the BIA superintendent, Stanley David Lyman, and his area director, Wyman Babby, both of whom were charged with acting in collusion with Wilson to keep him in power and maintain the hated form of government that favored the few and oppressed the many.

In this book—Superintendent Lyman's running account of the tense events of the siege, as he saw them—one of the most important and hitherto missing perspectives of Wounded Knee II is now supplied. Read in conjunction with two frank, enormously detailed, and little-known narratives—*The Innocent Victims of the Occupation of Wounded Knee, South Dakota v. the United States* (December 3, 1979) and the *Defendant's Requested Findings of Fact and Brief to the Trial Commissioner* (February 1981), prepared by the U.S. Department of Justice as legal briefs in a case before the U.S. Court of Claims—the reader acquires a wealth of insights into what happened among those who were doing the besieging.

Lyman's narrative on its own conveys an overwhelming picture of government confusion, bad communication, rivalries for turf, mixed motives, abysmal ignorance, bureaucratic ineptitude, and lack of understanding of the issues and depth of the appeal of those who were besieged. To some, Lyman, the relatively new and well-meaning superintendent at Pine Ridge, will appear as a terribly frustrated and tragic figure— a helpless swimmer hanging onto a piece of flotsam (his own view of what should have been done at Pine Ridge) in a stormy sea while battleships fire furious salvos at each other over his head.

With the best of motives but doomed again and again to be ignored and left out of things, Lyman, a gentle and honest

man, made no bones about his understood duties and obligations as a BIA superintendnet of the early 1970s, that is, to
support and assist the elected tribal leader, whoever he or she
may have been and no matter what some of the people may
have thought about it. "Now, whether the tribal president is
corrupt or not, as they say he is, is rather beside the issue.
This is a matter of revolution!" he declared at one point.

As the siege dragged on he began to see, or sense, things
that added to his frustration. Everyone in the government,
he knew, wanted the siege to end, and to end peaceably as
soon as possible. Everyone in the government wanted to bring
to justice those who had broken federal laws. But what he
seems not to have recognized fully and clearly is that from the
start, the highest levels in the White House—probably John
Ehrlichman on orders from President Nixon, and certainly
the president's close adviser, Leonard Garment, and his assistant, Bradley Patterson—were calling the shots. The orders
went down through the Department of Justice for a peaceful
solution. Aware of the sympathy for Indians that had been
newly aroused among the media and the general public, the
president did not want an Indian Attica. Extreme patience,
moderation and tolerance, the tiring out of the occupiers of
Wounded Knee, and adopting the policies followed successfully at Alcatraz and at the takeover of the BIA building—
these were the official prescription.

Lyman was not made a party to the ramifications of this
policy. At the same time, he also went through moments of
understanding of what lay behind the confrontation, which
added to his frustration and confusion. He was deeply touched
by an Indian who broke into tears as he tried to explain to
the superintendent what "the revolution" was all about. "As
he talked," Lyman confessed, "I realized that this man" had
"known for a long time what I" had "come to know only in the
last few months: that tribal government is an overlay; it does
not reach the people. He described the situation better, more
clearly than I had seen it for myself." Again, later, he heard it
from Ramon Roubideaux, AIM's lawyer. Lyman recounted:

"The Indian Reorganization Act [which had imposed the contested form of government on the people of Pine Ridge] is a tragic failure, he claimed; it is not responsive to Indians. Congress must repeal the IRA and allow Indians to go back to the Indian system. These oppressed people will not live under this form of government: they would rather die. There is no communication with Indians by the government; we need a forum in which the Indians can voice their concerns and complaints."

What did the occupiers of Wounded Knee want? Probably a return to the traditional *tiyospaye*—self-government under local or district traditional chiefs, headmen, and respected spiritual leaders. Lyman, perhaps, was unable to fathom such a system, or if he did, he felt it would be impractical. So throughout his narrative we see his dutiful attempts to carry out the responsibilities of a new-age BIA, giving his support to Dick Wilson and the duly elected majority of the tribal council—and, of course, solidifying a belief among his enemies that he was giving orders to and directing Wilson, as well as buttressing Wilson's power and position. In addition, pegged publicly as a Wilson ally, he was shunted aside by the Justice Department, which regarded Wilson as the problem rather than the solution. The blame, perhaps, lay in Washington, where the White House told the Justice Department to follow a particular course of action and the Department of the Interior failed to enlighten the Bureau of Indian Affairs of the official course being pursued. But remember that at the time, Rogers Morton, the secretary of the interior, was in California undergoing treatment for cancer and that the Bureau of Indian Affairs, still in disarray, had just lost its assistant secretary in charge of Indian affairs, Harrison Loesch, and its commissioner, Louis Bruce, both of whom had been fired by the White House.

In all, therefore, this is a very human document of an "odd man out" in great personal travail. One may wonder what Lyman's course would have been if orders had come down from the BIA explaining to him the White House's policy and the need to get in the same ballpark with the Justice Department. This did not happen, however, and so Lyman was left to stew and fret over seemingly unexplainable conduct in the handling of the crisis.

Within that context, his narrative is nevertheless a very valuable addition to the documentation of the confrontation. Lyman was faithful and frank in reporting events as he saw and understood them. He was a good observer, and he apparently never hesitated to reveal his private emotions and feelings. (He noted, for example, that he could not "keep back the hatred and the glee" when he saw Russell Means in handcuffs.) Moreover, he corroborated many of the behind-the-scenes revelations in the Department of Justice briefs (the tense gun-to-gun confrontation between the chief of the U.S. marshals and one of Dick Wilson's men at the roadblock, for instance), and he revealed a lot more that had never been told. (One would wish, however, that he had explained the offhand comment "Ablard [an associate deputy attorney general] was the one who blew the first negotiations with AIM.")

In many ways Wounded Knee II, a tragedy to so many people, was a watershed in modern-day Indian affairs. It gave new pride and strength to Indians all over the United States, including thousands of all ages and both sexes who, though not condoning the violence and unwilling to get involved in overt antigovernment activities, were inspired by what went on there. An entire generation of young Indians suddenly found voice and methods to attack unresponsive leaders on their reservations and to raise the decibel level of their demands for self-determination. Indian leadership as a whole changed, and from the change emerged many new, responsible leaders who pressed for the recognition of treaty rights, took the offensive against injustices and prejudice, entered into court cases for the long-neglected recognition of what rightfully belonged to their people, and achieved the passage of a self-determination act that, among other things, permitted them, through contracting, to assume the management and control of many of their affairs.

Pine Ridge, as well as other reservations, still unfortunately knows poverty and many of the other ills and grievances that existed before Wounded Knee II. But for every Pine Ridge there is a reservation that benefited from the confrontation. And across the country there are American Indians whose regained pride in their Indianness and in their own tribal heritage stems from the events that so disturbed and frustrated Stanley Lyman in those trying days of 1973.

Introduction

On the twenty-seventh of February, 1973, Wounded Knee, South Dakota, a tiny village on the Pine Ridge Indian Reservation, was occupied by a militant group of American Indians who called themselves the American Indian Movement. That occupation lasted for several months during tortuous times of political upheaval in the United States. Even during the struggle over Watergate, the Wounded Knee occupation vied well in the national news for the attention of the American people. The continuing violence disrupted every aspect of life on the Pine Ridge Reservation and created bitter divisions among its people, the Oglala Sioux Tribe.

Wounded Knee II was the culmination of a long and difficult period for American Indians, who were impatient with the lack of both economic and social progress. As part of that impatience and discontent, the American Indian Movement, or AIM, as it is commonly called, was organized in 1968 in Minneapolis, Minnesota, by Dennis H. Banks and Clyde Bellecourt, both Chippewa Indians. By the time of the Wounded Knee occupation, AIM claimed 300,000 members in forty-three cities nationwide. Like Banks and Bellecourt, most of the AIM leaders, and many of its members as well, had lived the urban experience in America. Russell Means, who played the central role in the Wounded Knee upheaval, was raised in California. Though a member of the Oglala Sioux Tribe, his experience on the Pine Ridge Reservation was brief and recent. Many writers have assumed that the movement led by these powerful, charismatic young men in their thirties and early forties was copied from the student movement and black civil rights movements and as such was part of the general milieu of the political dislocation that attended the era of the Vietnam War. Certainly many of the methods, activities, and attitudes of AIM have recognizable counterparts in those other groups. But the organization also found support in other quarters: from some reservation Indians, even those of older generations, who saw in AIM a glimmer of hope for the restoration of a way of life long past. An AIM slogan of 1973 proclaimed, "The Red Giant is on one knee, but he is getting ready to stand up."

The occupation of Wounded Knee was preceded by a long chain of AIM activities, some constructive in purpose and outcome, but most violent and disruptive. The organization and its leaders rose in the estimation of many Oglala Sioux on the Pine Ridge Reservation because of its prompt and vigorous action following the murder of a man from the tribe. On February 13, 1972, Raymond Yellow Thunder was beaten to death by a group of whites in nearby Gordon, Nebraska. AIM leaders led a band of 250 Pine Ridge Reservation Indians to Gordon for a confrontation with the town's mayor. They quickly won most of their demands, and convictions in the case were ultimately obtained. The AIM leaders and their marchers returned to Pine Ridge as heroes in the eyes of many. AIM gained national attention again in November of 1972 when some of its leaders and members marched on the Bureau of Indian Affairs building in Washington, D.C., occupied it forcibly, and ransacked its files and offices. In the months between this occupation and that of Wounded Knee, the South Dakota area saw increasing unrest and disorder fomented by AIM. During the first two weeks of February 1973, units of the South Dakota National Guard were called into active duty in Rapid City, Custer, and other locations, and the U.S. Marshal Service sent 105 deputies into the Pine Ridge Reservation to ensure against violence there. The events of the night of February 27 were thus prefaced by a long preparation.

It was no accident that the site of the most dramatic AIM disorder should be Wounded Knee. The locality of Wounded Knee is a powerful symbol in the minds of American Indians. It was there in 1890 that an Indian revivalist movement referred to by the whites as the Ghost Dance caused fear and anger in the U.S. Army. On December 29 an encampment of Sioux at Wounded Knee Creek was surrounded by a unit of the U.S. Seventh Cavalry. Four Hotchkiss guns were positioned on the surrounding hills, and the Indians were ordered to surrender their arms. As the men began piling up their rifles, a shot went off, and the Hotchkiss guns opened fire. What followed was a massacre in which approximately 150 Indians— men, women, and children—were killed and an additional 50 wounded. Subsequently, perhaps as many as 100 more froze to death in the bitter weather on the Oglala lands where they had fled from the army. The dead were buried in a single mass grave, which in 1973 was located behind Sacred Heart Catholic Church in Wounded Knee. To the army it was the last battle of the Plains Indian wars, and eighteen Congressional Medals of Honor were awarded to participating soldiers. To the Sioux it is a wound that has not healed across the generations. Leo Wilcox, an Oglala Sioux tribal councilman who figures prominently in the first part of this narrative, remarked to newsmen just a few days before his death that the Sioux will not rest until those Medals of Honor are revoked.

The Wounded Knee incident took place within the context of long-established federal-Indian policy. According to the Supreme Court, the Indian tribes of the United States are "domestic dependent nations." The word "dependent" means that they are wards of the government of the United States. Their lands are held in trust by the U.S. government through the secretary of the interior and the subdivision of that cabinet office called the Bureau of Indian Affairs (BIA). The Bureau has been one of the most vilified of all the government agencies in the history of the nation, but in spite of the constant attacks, it has, historically, represented the will of Congress and often of the president. In each of the major reservations in the United States, the Bureau places a superintendent to run the federal programs, to provide assistance to Indian tribes, and to act as an on-the-spot representative for the trustee relationship with the federal government.

From 1887 until 1934 it was the official policy of the U.S. government to try to Christianize, agrarianize, and civilize the native population. Most historians agree that these processes were a colossal failure. In 1934 the policy was reversed in the Wheeler-Howard Act, also called the Indian Reorganization Act. Indian religion and languages were to be respected; increasing respect for Indian self-rule was to be the creed of the Bureau of Indian Affairs and the policy of the United States government. But this policy was short lived. During the 1950s Congress decided to terminate the special relationship between Indian tribes and the federal government as rapidly as possible, and a few tribes were actually terminated. This policy, too, resulted in additional dislocation and despair in the Indian community. By the time President Kennedy took over in 1961, this process was halted.

In the late 1960s and early 1970s, the concept of self-determination was becoming the watchword for American Indian tribes who were hoping to gain a greater degree of control over their own local affairs. In 1969 President Nixon made self-determination an official policy of the federal government, and the Bureau of Indian Affairs, acting as the Department of the Interior's representative on Indian reservations, had begun to have a changing role in American Indian life. There was ambiguity about the extent of the federal trusteeship. Tribal councils became increasingly militant in their demands for independence from the control of the Bureau, and the Bureau, especially the progressives within it, saw themselves and their staffs as the friends of the elected councils on Indian reservations. Pine Ridge Reservation certainly had such a man representing the new philosophy in its superintendent, Stanley David Lyman.

Yet the role of the superintendent, the power of the BIA, and the very nature of tribal government were issues underlying, at least partially, the Wounded Knee takeover. On December 14, 1935, the Oglala Sioux Tribe had voted to accept self-government under the terms of the Indian Reorganization Act. It adopted as its constitution a document that was written by Felix Cohen, a lawyer for the Department of the Interior, and that was accepted by many other tribes as well. The constitution calls for a tribal government made up of a president or chairman, an executive committee, and a tribal council. At the Pine Ridge Reservation the tribal council consisted of twenty members from eight districts, each elected for a two-year term. In 1973 the president of the Oglala Sioux Tribe, also serving a two-year term, was Dick Wilson, aged 38, a plumber by trade and father of six children. The executive committee was composed of Dave Long, vice president; Toby Eagle Bull, secretary; Emma T. Nelson, treasurer; and Everett Lone Hill, fifth member.

The referendum vote to accept self-government and the new constitution had been very close in 1935, and a sizable minority of Oglalas remained strongly opposed to it. That group formed the core of a faction of discontent and opposition which was still very much in existence in 1973. Tribal government at Pine Ridge was split between the supporters of Dick Wilson and those against him. Those opposed to the chairman included Vice President Dave Long; a number of tribal councilmen, including Dick Little, Hobart Keith, and Birgil Kills Straight; the Oglala Sioux Civil Rights Organization; and AIM itself. From the time Dick Wilson took office in April 1972, until February 1973, there had been three attempts to impeach him, all unsuccessful. A major demand of AIM throughout the occupation of Wounded Knee was that Dick Wilson be removed from office, that Stan Lyman be removed as superintendent, and that the tribal constitution be abolished.

These internal struggles exacerbated an already complex situation of conflicting and overlapping authority and jurisdiction—a situation stemming from the particular relationship between an Indian tribe and the federal government. In response to the Wounded Knee occupation, federal officials and negotiators had to face serious and delicate questions: How much power did the tribal council have in attempting to remove the Indians, non-Indians, and locals who had occupied Wounded Knee? Should police power be used by the BIA? Should the FBI exercise its usual jurisdiction over such matters? As this narrative reveals, the various federal agencies brought together to resolve the Wounded Knee crisis did not have the same answers to these questions. A unifying thread running throughout Lyman's personal account of these events is his unrelenting efforts to support the elected officials of the Oglala Sioux Tribe and to protect the interests and prerogatives of tribal government from any encroachment by the federal establishment.

One of the problems to afflict the tribal council was a split between those of mixed-blood Sioux ancestry and those who were full-bloods. The full-bloods felt that those of mixed ancestry were too close to the white establishment and that basic Sioux interests and culture were compromised. The mixed-bloods were often viewed as far more articulate in dealing with the outside world, and they, in turn, often thought of the full-bloods as less able to accommodate to a rapidly changing society and economy. This oversimplistic analysis of the struggle at least allows the reader to understand that a trenchant and long-enduring contest was present along with the other issues at Wounded Knee.

Stanley David Lyman became the superintendent of the Bureau of Indian Affairs agency at Pine Ridge in 1972. Lyman was a native of South Dakota and had been raised in the Quaker tradition. He grew up on a ranch in western South Dakota on the edge of the Black Hills. During the Great Depression he attended Yankton College in South Dakota, receiving a bachelor's degree in English. He later took a master's degree in education from Colorado Teacher's College.

During World War II, Lyman, fluent in Spanish, worked for the War Food Administration bringing Mexican laborers from Mexico to work in the fields while "our boys" were overseas. After a stint at ranching, he began his career in the Bureau of Indian Affairs as an employee of the Relocation Program, which provided American Indians with urban employment and education during the 1950s. His work was at the Pine Ridge Reservation; in Aberdeen, South Dakota; and in Denver and Chicago. In 1941 Stanley married June Kremer, who was a teacher and counselor in various Indian schools.

Following highly successful appointments as the superintendent of the Fort Peck Reservation in Montana and the Uintah-Ouray reservation in Utah, he was sent to Pine Ridge with the express purpose of creating an economic revival in this impoverished area, as he had been able to do in Utah. The initial stages of this work had begun when the occupation of Wounded Knee occurred.

Lyman was a practical man in implementing programs, yet as a BIA worker he was always an idealist. His idealism was reinforced by his wife; both represented that deep loyalty to community and country that is far less present in recent times. To most who knew Stan, he was a powerfully appealing person. Thus, the following document is not to be considered an adequate reflection of the total man; at that juncture of his life he was frustrated and angry. The depth of that frustration, as expressed in this manuscript, reflects as well the anguish of other dedicated personnel of the BIA. The Sioux community in which they were attempting to work is also shown at a time of incredible stress and struggle.

As a friend of the Lymans, I phoned after Wounded Knee was occupied to see whether they were safe and well. In the course of the conversation I asked Stan if he had been able to document the history of the events. He muttered something about time to collect his wits. I pressed him to tape-record his thoughts every night. He tried. In a few days he called and said the process would be easier if he had an audience. It was then I asked him to make me his audience. "Speak to me, Stan," I advised him. Hence, the book that follows is far more than just an editing job to me.

Stanley Lyman's record of the Wounded Knee crisis begins on February 22, 1973, with the tribal council meeting at which the impeachment of Chairman Dick Wilson was the central issue. He recorded for two days and then, with the press of events and responsibilities, was unable to resume his account until March 27. During the intervening month a great many things occurred, not all of which Stanley was able to include in his summary account of the takeover and the first weeks of occupation. To provide continuity and background for the events to follow, the major occurrences of that thirty-one day period will be presented here.

The impeachment proceedings of February 23 broke up in disorder, to reconvene the following day. Threats having been made against the life of Chairman Wilson, the federal marshals placed him and his family under protective custody. The object of similar threats, Superintendent Lyman nevertheless declined the offer of protection and went home to sleep in his own bed. The next day, February 24, the tribal council reconvened, and its members voted fourteen to zero, with one abstaining, to dismiss the impeachment charges against Dick Wilson. The chairman and his family were released from protective custody in an atmosphere of watchful waiting.

Threatening statements from AIM leaders about caravans of followers and imminent "AIM action" in Pine Ridge were taken fully seriously by the marshals and the FBI, so Stan Lyman was requested not to attend the funeral of Ben Black Elk, which was held Monday, February 26, in the town of Manderson. Black Elk had been a distinguished elder and medicine man of the Oglala Sioux Tribe, and in his honor the BIA office was closed Monday for a day of mourning. The superintendent was dressed up and prepared to go to the funeral, but the marshals considered it too great a risk. Stan Lyman, like Dick Wilson, they said, was prime hostage material.

Following Black Elk's funeral, 150 Indians assembled at Calico Hall, a frequent meeting site for AIM. The group was reportedly split over a proposed confrontation at the BIA building in Pine Ridge. Russell Means favored a passive approach, and Vernon Bellecourt, the brother of Clyde Bellecourt, favored an aggressive stand. No agreement was reached. The next day, Tuesday, February 27, about 200 AIM members and supporters met again at Calico Hall, many of them armed with rifles, shotguns, pistols, and knives. In the evening they formed a caravan, ostensibly heading for the town of Porcupine and a larger meeting hall. Instead, the caravan stopped at the village of Wounded Knee, took over the town at gunpoint, raided the trading post, ransacked the museum, and took eleven residents prisoner, including Father Paul Manhardt, the Jesuit priest at Sacred Heart Catholic Church. The takeover was described by an observer from the press as "a commando raid in the most accurate sense: well organized, lightning fast, and executed in almost total darkness" (*Rapid City Journal*, March 1, 1973, p. 1).

More than one hundred law-enforcement officials from the FBI, the BIA police, and the U.S. Marshal Service quickly surrounded the area and established roadblocks on the four roads into Wounded Knee. Shots were fired from within Wounded Knee at oncoming vehicles and at the roadblocks, the bridge over Wounded Knee Creek was burned, and the occupiers began to set up fortifications. One casualty resulted from the gunfire: a young man, seventeen years old, in the occupying force lost his hand when a rifle exploded. He was evacuated out of Wounded Knee by BIA firemen and taken to a hospital.

The following day, February 28, Carter Camp, a Pawnee from Ponca City, Oklahoma, and a national coordinator for AIM, presented the demands of the occupiers: that the Senate committee headed by Senator Edward Kennedy launch an immediate investigation of the BIA and the Department of the Interior for their handling of the affairs of the Oglala Sioux Tribe; that Senator William Fulbright investigate the 371 treaties between the federal government and the Indians to show how the government had failed to live up to those treaties; that the Oglala Sioux be allowed to elect new leaders, from among the ranks of the traditionalists, not, as Camp said, puppets like now in office; and that state and local governments become more sensitive to Indian problems. The hostages were declared to be in no immediate danger unless the area was stormed by police, but it was made clear that the occupation of Wounded Knee would be maintained by force. "We have the men and the weapons to hold it," declared Camp. "We are not going to give in without a fight" (*Rapid City Journal*, February 28, 1973, p. 2).

Tribal President Wilson issued an official written statement that same day condemning the takeover as a criminal act—an attempt at mob rule and the overthrow of the legitimate tribal government by individuals who had "assumed self-appointed positions . . . as leaders of the Oglala Sioux people. . . . The current crisis on this reservation, as created by members of the AIM organization, and instigated by a small group of chronic complainers [on the reservation], which infects every community, is certainly causing annoyance, disgust and concern among the overwhelming majority of the Oglala Sioux on this reservation." The statement concluded with the request that the leaders of the takeover "be held liable for their actions and prosecuted to the fullest extent of the law." This was the beginning of a hard-line attitude on the part of the tribal government toward the insurgents—a position that was constantly ignored by the Justice Department representatives throughout the months of the occupation.

Federal officials moved quickly to establish a framework for dealing with the crisis. William Clayton, U.S. attorney for South Dakota, had already set up headquarters in the BIA building at Pine Ridge, as Stan Lyman described in his entry for February 22. Throughout the day of February 28 the government roadblocks took fire from Indian snipers positioned in the surrounding hills. Ralph Erickson, special assistant to the U.S. attorney general, was sent from Washington to serve as the ranking official on the scene from the Department of Justice. He was accompanied by Wayne Colburn, director of the U.S. Marshal Service. They arrived at Gordon, Nebraska, about midnight.

On Thursday, March 1, Erickson met with the Justice Department personnel already at Pine Ridge, established a chain of command under which the three law-enforcement agencies represented there—the U.S. Marshal Service, the FBI, and the BIA police—would operate, and instructed them to exercise restraint in the use of deadly force. The two senators from South Dakota, James Abourezk and George McGovern, arrived that morning, accompanied by representatives from the offices of Senators Kennedy and Fulbright. Their purpose was not to negotiate the demands of the occupiers but to ascertain the safety of the hostages and to work for their release. They met in the afternoon with AIM representatives at one of the roadblocks outside Wounded Knee. Another session was held that night, from eight o'clock until midnight, at the home of one of the hostage families inside Wounded Knee.

The senators described their role as one of mainly listening to the grievances of the insurgents, but AIM did agree to work with representatives of the Justice Department to establish a cease-fire. They assured the senators that the hostages were free to leave the area but that they had elected to stay in Wounded Knee because that was their home. The senators talked to the hostages themselves and offered to take them out with them; the hostages declined. Satisfied that the hostage situation was resolved, the senators left the reservation.

The next two days saw no real progress toward ending the takeover or even toward establishing meaningful negotiations. The optimism expressed by Senators Abourezk and McGovern for an early end to the crisis quickly faded. Gunfire directed at the federal roadblocks continued sporadically but persistently, and Ralph Erickson, ranking Justice Department representative, said he was not satisfied that the hostages were indeed free. Erickson characterized the initial talks with AIM leaders as "not very promising" (*Rapid City Journal*, March 3, 1973, p. 1).

On the morning of Saturday, March 3, a team of six attorneys requested by AIM were allowed to pass through the federal roadblocks. They conferred with the occupiers and then participated in negotiations with Justice Department representatives later that day. A key issue in the negotiations of March 3 and 4 was the nature of the criminal charges to be brought against the insurgents and who would be charged.

The AIM representatives and their lawyers insisted that charges be filed only against AIM leaders and that these not include charges for kidnapping. Russell Means said, "I can see two or three years in jail, but I can't see seventeen years," referring to the minimum sentence for kidnapping in South Dakota.

Late Sunday afternoon, March 4, Ralph Erickson, in consultation with and with the approval of U.S. Attorney General Richard Kleindienst, presented the government's proposal to end the armed standoff. Beginning at 8:00 A.M. on Monday, March 5, all nonresidents of Wounded Knee would be allowed to leave the area, subject to certain conditions. All men, but not women and children, must identify themselves to the personnel at the roadblocks as they departed. They could neither carry weapons nor approach the checkpoints with weapons. Arrangements would be made for them to leave their weapons with identification if they owned them and wished to recover them later. As long as the departure was orderly, no arrests would be made and no charges would be filed against any of the participants withdrawing in this manner, pending the findings of a federal grand jury. All those wishing to leave Wounded Knee under these conditions had to do so by 6:00 Monday evening. Once nonresidents of Wounded Knee had left the area, and provided there was no further violence, there would be no reason for the federal peacekeeping forces to maintain the present guard. The roadblocks would then be taken down and free access to the village restored.

Tribal President Dick Wilson was not consulted about the terms of the proposal, and he denounced it as a virtual offer of amnesty to those who had taken up arms against the government. He repeated his stand that this was an internal problem of the Oglala Sioux Tribe and that if justice was to prevail, it must be settled by the Oglala Sioux Tribe itself, without interference from "foreign Indians" or the Justice Department of the United States.

The government proposal was handed to AIM attorneys by

Ralph Erickson Sunday evening. When the proposal was read in the AIM camp that night, it was jeered, and the paper on which it was written was burned. AIM leaders declared that they would not leave the area or lay down their arms and asked to negotiate for a flow of supplies through the road-blocks.

Negotiations continued Monday, March 5, in a ceremonial tepee erected on the Big Foot Trail between the federal road-blocks and the AIM perimeter. No Indians left Wounded Knee that day, but Ralph Erickson, encouraged by the tenor of the negotiations, extended the offer for departure to include the daylight hours of Tuesday, March 6. To give the Indians every possible chance it was extended again to Wednesday and, finally, to Thursday evening, March 8. All the while, negotia-tions continued, with the Indians broadening their demands and the federal negotiators becoming ever more conciliatory. Although only a few of the occupiers accepted the offer to leave without immediate arrest, Erickson and his negotiators felt that an agreement was near. But when it became clear that the federal government could and would accept the AIM demands, those demands were shifted to something abso-lutely unacceptable, and the hope of agreement slipped away.

Once again the crux of the matter was the government of the Oglala Sioux Tribe. The occupiers demanded that the Department of the Interior remove Wilson as president, sus-pend the tribal council, and revoke the tribal constitution. Of course the Department of the Interior would not counte-nance such a thing, and it had no legal authority to do this, even if it had been willing to. Negotiations broke down, and it was announced that the free-departure offer would expire Thursday evening and would not be renewed. As quoted by the Associated Press on March 7, Ralph Erickson said of the negotiations, "I cannot escape the feeling that the [AIM] leaders are bent on one of two courses: total capitulation by the U.S. government to their illegal demands or violence" (*Minot Daily News*, March 7, 1973).

In the gravity of the situation, Erickson again urged those

inside the Wounded Knee perimeter, both residents and non-residents, to leave by nightfall Thursday. Several groups of women and children did leave: forty-two individuals on Wednesday and another fifty on Thursday, all reported to be residents of the village. Inside the AIM camp there was talk of what many there believed to be imminent attack by federal peacekeeping forces. Tension increased as the time neared for the end of the free-departure period. Despite the fact that a cease-fire was in effect, gunfire broke out between a patrol of Indians outside of the village and a government emplacement. Two Indians were wounded in the skirmish—one in the hand, the other in the leg. Neither left the AIM stronghold for medical attention; they were taken instead to the Catholic church, which served as an infirmary, and treated there. Leonard Crow Dog, a medicine man from the Rosebud Sioux Reservation, removed the bullet from the leg wound.

Negotiations resumed Friday, March 9, amidst Erickson's assurances that the Justice Department would "make every effort to arrive at a peaceful conclusion to the tense and dangerous situation" (*New York Times*, March 8, 1973). Erickson himself had returned to Washington, leaving Charles D. Ablard, deputy assistant U.S. attorney general, as the ranking Justice Department official on the scene. In long sessions Ablard and Ramon Roubideaux, AIM's attorney, worked on a fifteen-point proposal made by representatives of the National Council of Churches of Christ. This group had been in Pine Ridge since early in the confrontation and often acted as an unofficial intermediary between the government and the Indians.

For the second time in as many days, an agreement seemed near. Justice Department officials announced at a press briefing that the two sides had reached "an agreement in principle"; all that remained to be settled were the manner and time in which the occupiers of Wounded Knee would leave. As negotiations continued into the night, Ablard asked that the occupiers depart by Sunday, March 11. Roubideaux asked that the date be set at Monday instead. Ablard agreed, and it appeared that the settlement was firm. Once again, however, the AIM leaders would not agree to what their attorneys had negotiated, and once again they countered with new and broader demands.

Swept aside in the federal maneuvering to end the crisis, Dick Wilson and the tribal council nevertheless attempted positive steps of their own. On Wednesday, March 7, Wilson issued a detailed statement to the press setting forth some of the problems at the Pine Ridge Reservation and offering concrete measures to attack them. He decried the attention and recognition the federal government and the press had given to a militant and destructive element on the reservation at the expense of the legitimate tribal government: "We call out to all Congressional, federal, state, and local interests to hear the voice of the Oglala Sioux Tribe and assist us in dealing with our many problems." He concluded by stating that the Department of the Interior, through the General Accounting Office of the United States, would provide "a complete and thorough audit of all Tribal finances and accounting activities." This measure had been requested by the tribal council at the conclusion of the impeachment hearings against Wilson himself. In addition, Wilson said that he had personally contacted Marvin Franklin, assistant to the secretary of the interior for Indian affairs; Franklin had promised to come to Pine Ridge as soon as possible to confer with the tribal council. On Thursday, March 8, the tribal court ordered that all nonmembers of the tribe be evicted from the reservation. As will be seen in Stan Lyman's narrative, the matter of jurisdiction and the enforcement of the orders of the tribal court emerged as increasingly difficult problems in the weeks to come.

On March 10 a major concession was made by the federal government in an effort to put an end to the on-again, off-again agreements and to effect a real settlement: government roadblocks would be withdrawn. This measure was announced by Ablard to the various agencies and officials at Pine Ridge at a morning briefing meeting. In his office notes for that day, Lyman wrote that the decision to withdraw the roadblocks was made by Ablard and Wayne Colburn, director of the U.S. Marshal Service, and that it had been cleared through the highest levels of the Justice Department and by the White House as well. The secretary of the interior and the BIA were against it, but they were overruled, he said. Now Lyman, as superintendent at Pine Ridge, was forced to "sell it to the tribe," as he put it—to convince the elected leadership of the Oglala Sioux to accept a decision that had already been made. This was a position he was put in frequently during the months of the occupation of Wounded Knee, and one he disliked and disapproved of.

In principle, the decision to withdraw the roadblocks was not an unreasonable one. Throughout the negotiations of Friday, March 9, AIM had asked for reduction of the government forces around Wounded Knee and for removal of the armored personnel carriers. The explanation offered by AIM leaders for not accepting the Monday withdrawal date agreed on by Ablard and Roubideaux was that they feared they would be gunned down if they approached the government emplacements unarmed. Wayne Colburn met with Stanley Holder, designated as head of security inside the AIM camp, to ascertain what AIM's response would be if the roadblocks were removed. Holder promised that in return, the occupiers would withdraw from their fortifications and would permit free movement into and out of Wounded Knee. This offer was accepted, and the government withdrawal began at about two o'clock Saturday afternoon. The roadblocks and armored personnel carriers were removed, and surveillance was maintained by agents with binoculars from automobiles placed several miles outside the perimeter. Ralph Erickson issued a press release in Washington, announcing, "We are doing this because we believe this is the proper step at this point in moving toward a peaceful resolution."

The response within the AIM fortress to the government withdrawal was not, however, the long-sought resolution that federal officials had been led to expect. Instead, AIM leaders claimed victory over the federal establishment. "We have won this war," proclaimed Dennis Banks at a victory rally inside Wounded Knee, "but there are other wars to come. We have a war in Washington State; we have a war in Pawnee, Oklahoma. All these wars are next, and the FBI and the Justice Department better lay their plans for these" (*New York Times*, March 11, 1973, p. 3).

The federal forces in Pine Ridge watched and waited. Late in the afternoon, after the federal withdrawal was accomplished, two FBI agents approached Wounded Knee by car to determine whether the occupiers had withdrawn. To all appearances there had been no change. The next day, March 11, around seven o'clock in the morning, FBI agents again approached Wounded Knee to verify whether it was in fact an open area as promised. They were turned back with threats and pointed rifles.

Later that morning several U.S. postal inspectors, who had heard the area was now open, went to Wounded Knee to ascertain the condition of the village's post office. The six men were detained at gunpoint, searched, and held prisoner for two hours. Then they were marched out of the village by armed Indian guards and driven by truck to an AIM roadblock, still manned and armed, contrary to the agreement. They were ordered out of the truck and lined up on the roadside with their hands on their heads. After a time they were allowed to march off one by one to their vehicle, a quarter of a mile down the road. In another incident that day, two ranchers were similarly "arrested" by the insurgents, tied to chairs, and held prisoner for several hours. The most serious incident occurred north of the village when FBI agent Curtis A. Fitzgerald was wounded by armed Indians firing from a van as they entered Wounded Knee. He suffered gunshot wounds to the right forearm and the left hand.

Inside Wounded Knee, Russell Means, talking over a loudspeaker to the occupiers, proclaimed Wounded Knee an independent nation and threatened that any federal official attempting to enter the area would be shot on sight: "If any foreign official representing any foreign power—specifically, the United States—comes in here, it will be treated as an act of war and dealt with accordingly." Dennis Banks declared, "We're going to establish here a symbolic Indian government, and we're going to stay here indefinitely. We expect Indians from all over the country to help us demonstrate our ability to rule ourselves" (*New York Times*, March 12, 1973).

Indeed, Indians as well as armed young whites did come in support of the AIM insurgents. By Monday, March 12, the number of dissidents inside Wounded Knee had doubled because of the free access to the area allowed by the removal of the federal guard points. The AIM ranks, which until then had numbered about two hundred, were increased to about four hundred, and additional supplies and ammunition were also brought in.

The government was thus forced to reevaluate its position. At 2:00 P.M., Monday, March 12, Ralph Erickson announced from Washington that the federal roadblocks would be reimposed around Wounded Knee and that access to the area would be restricted "as long as necessary to restore order" (*New York Times*, March 13, 1973). By 5:30 that evening, the guard points were again in place. A negotiating session planned for that day was canceled. A member of the Community Relations Service division of the Justice Department met briefly with AIM's representative, Stanley Holder, saying, "I have been instructed to tell you that because of what has happened, the government does not feel you have been negotiating in good faith, and there is no reason to have a meeting today" (*New York Times*, March 13, 1973). Holder answered that any agreements entered into previously had been made while the AIM leaders were American citizens and were invalid now that Wounded Knee was an independent nation.

It appeared that the government had entered a new phase in its handling of the crisis. D. Harlington Wood, assistant attorney general, Civil Division, arrived from Washington to take over from Ablard as ranking official of the Justice Department. Public-information officers from the Department of Justice who had served as government spokesmen at Pine Ridge were joined by information officers from the Department of the Interior. A federal grand jury convened in Sioux Falls, South Dakota, to hear evidence in the take-over of Wounded Knee and to issue indictments based on that evidence.

Harlington Wood moved quickly to reestablish direct nego-tiations with AIM. The afternoon of Tuesday, March 13, he met with the six "elected councilmen" of the new nation of Wounded Knee: Dennis Banks, Russell Means, Clyde Belle-court, Carter Camp, Pedro Bissonette, and Vernon Long. A key issue in these negotiations was the Indians' demand, voiced in earlier sessions as well, that the highest ranking official of the Department of the Interior directly involved with Indian affairs come to Pine Ridge and meet personally with them. That official was Marvin Franklin, assistant sec-retary of the interior and acting head of the BIA. Franklin, himself an Indian and a former tribal chairman of the Iowa Indian Nation, was a man whom Stanley Lyman respected and admired. As will be seen in Lyman's account, Franklin played a determinative role at a very crucial stage in the crisis. The Department of the Interior had held firm in its stand that no such meeting would take place until the Indians laid down their arms and vacated Wounded Knee.

That same day, Tuesday, March 13, the Oglala Sioux Tribal Council met for the first time since the Wounded Knee takeover. Fourteen of the twenty members were present, con-stituting a quorum. These fourteen members voted unani-mously to add a removal clause to the already existing exclusion powers that the tribe held by virtue of its consti-tution. The resolution stated that when a state of emergency existed on the reservation, nonresidents of the reservation could be evicted by tribal police or by any federal officer. This resolution gave permanent authority to the court order issued March 8 by the tribal court. It was signed and approved by Superintendent Lyman on March 16 and put into action almost immediately.

A blizzard hit Pine Ridge on Wednesday, March 14, piling up deep snowdrifts and making roads impassable. Negotiations were halted for two days because both the AIM camp and the federal officials were snowed in. Wednesday night and Thursday were described as the quietest yet. Harlington Wood, now the chief federal negotiator, returned to Washington on Thursday to confer with the heads of the Department of the Interior and the Department of Justice. This raised speculation that the White House was now becoming directly involved in the course of the negotiations and that Wood would return with instructions for the government's final offer. Negotiations were postponed pending his return on Friday night, March 16.

AIM's response to the government's gesture of withdrawing its roadblocks had caused a hardening of opinion toward the occupying force among federal officials. For instance, as quoted by the Associated Press on March 15, Senator George McGovern said that the time had come to arrest the occupiers: "Every reasonable effort at negotiation has failed; every concession made by the government has been matched with yet another American Indian Movement demand. We are at the point where we are either going to enforce the law or we are not. . . . The law must be enforced. Those who have broken the law must be arrested and pay the penalties under the law" (*Rapid City Journal*, March 15, 1973). In statements quoted by the Associated Press on March 16, Secretary of the Interior Rogers C. B. Morton defended his department's refusal to meet with the militants in an area held by illegal force of arms: "Nothing is gained by blackmail. You cannot run this government or find equitable solutions with a gun at your head or the head of a hostage. . . . Any agency of government that is forced into a fast deal by revolutionary tactics, blackmail, or terrorism is not worth its salt" (*El Paso Times*, March 16, 1973). The actions of the militants, Morton said, were "criminal operations and should be dealt with accordingly."

Indeed, these individuals were being dealt with by law-enforcement officials everywhere but inside Wounded Knee itself. Those caught attempting to enter or leave Wounded Knee were arrested and arraigned on federal charges such as burglary, larceny, and interfering with a law-enforcement officer in his correction of a civil disorder. A press release of March 13 listed the total number of arrests by the FBI, the U.S. marshals, and the BIA police at eighty-seven since the seige of Wounded Knee began on February 27. The federal grand jury, after two days of testimony, handed down thirteen sealed indictments against thirty-one persons in the occupying force. Again the charges were burglary, larceny, conspiracy, and civil disorder. No kidnapping charges were made, although testimony was heard from several of the eleven hostages.

In another conciliatory gesture, Justice Department representatives agreed to allow food, fuel, and medical supplies to be taken into the AIM fortress. Officials of the Community Relations Service and observers from the National Council of Churches accompanied such supplies into Wounded Knee on Thursday, March 15. They reported no emergency conditions existing in the village.

On Saturday afternoon, March 17, Harlington Wood met Dennis Banks and Ramon Roubideaux at the main federal roadblock outside Wounded Knee and delivered a sealed envelope containing twelve copies of a comprehensive proposal from the government. Wood said the document was not to be regarded as an ultimatum but as the government's best offer. The AIM leaders would be given as much time as they wanted to consider it, and he would return at any time to talk to them further.

The proposal offered a detailed plan for ending the confrontation. As a compromise solution to the Indians' demands that Marvin Franklin confer with them at Wounded Knee, the proposal stipulated that a meeting would be held between Franklin and AIM leaders in Sioux Falls. The AIM leaders would receive safe conduct to the meeting and would then submit peacefully to arrest afterward. As that session in Sioux Falls began, all weapons at Wounded Knee would be laid down in one location, identified for future recovery by their owners. All occupiers would go to a roadblock for identification and processing, and those with warrants against them would submit to arrest. Federal agents would not cross the perimeter into Wounded Knee for three hours after the laying down of arms. Other provisions dealt with the access to be allowed the press, the presence of federal officers on the reservation, the setting of bail, and other matters.

Marvin Franklin came to the Pine Ridge Reservation that day for the first time since the conflict began. He made it clear that he was there to confer with the tribal chairman and the tribal council, as he had promised Dick Wilson he would do, and not to negotiate with the militants.

Saturday night the federal emplacements again took fire and returned it. One of the occupiers, Rocky Madrid, a paramedic from San Luis, California, was grazed in the side by a rifle bullet.

The next day, Sunday, March 18, a press conference was held at the trading post inside Wounded Knee, and the government's proposal was denounced as "total capitulation and submission to arrest and disarmament." Stanley Holder, standing in front of a sign reading "Independent Oglala Sioux Nation," pledged continued resistance by a society of new warriors and ceremoniously burned the proposal. Harlington Wood and Wayne Colburn met with AIM leaders for nearly two hours concerning the proposal, but nothing was achieved.

The response from the militants came on Monday, March 19, in the form of a counterproposal that they termed their "final ultimatum" to the United States. They demanded that President Nixon name a special emissary from among the Sioux to negotiate with them a settlement based on the treaty rights of the Oglala Sioux Nation dating from 1868 and 1876.

The Justice Department negotiators offered certain compromises to encourage acceptance of the government proposal; one of these was that Marvin Franklin would meet with residents of Wounded Knee, but not nonresident occupiers, to discuss their grievances. No progress was seen in the negotiations of the day, and no definite arrangements were made for further sessions.

Harlington Wood left Pine Ridge on Tuesday, March 20, leaving Richard Hellstern, deputy assistant attorney general, as the ranking Justice Department official. It was made clear that the government's offers of March 18 and 19 still stood and that Hellstern would meet with AIM leaders at any time. Also, Franklin remained in Pine Ridge in case the offer of a meeting with Wounded Knee residents was accepted. With no response from AIM to either the Justice Department or the Interior Department, the next day Marvin Franklin, too, left for Washington.

In the midst of the stalemate in the armed confrontation, significant steps were being taken through government channels. On Monday, March 19, petitions were presented to Superintendent Lyman and to Charles Soller, associate solicitor of the Department of the Interior, by tribal councilmen Dick Little and Hobart Keith and by tribal members Delores Swift Bird, Barbara Means, and Louis Bad Wound. This petition, important in Lyman's narrative, called for a referendum election on whether to abolish the tribal constitution and with it the existing tribal government. The referendum movement led by those opposed to Dick Wilson and encouraged by AIM had gathered 1,450 signatures from members of the Oglala Sioux Tribe.

The petition reflected the split, mentioned several times by Lyman, between the full-blood traditionalists on the reservation, many of whom lived in the outlying areas, and the mixed-bloods of Pine Ridge, whose interests tribal government was seen to serve almost exclusively. Affiliation with one group or the other was more a matter of outlook and attitude than of ancestry, but the division was very real. Many of the 1,450 signatures came from the full-blood faction, those opposed to Dick Wilson and most likely to favor AIM.

The tribal constitution required that a referendum petition of this kind be made by one-third of the eligible voters of the tribe. The legal procedure, once the petition was submitted, was that the signatures would be verified over a fifteen-day period. If they were valid and ascertained to be of the correct proportion, then an election would be called by the secretary of the interior. If a majority of the people voted to revoke the tribal constitution, the measure would still have to be approved by the secretary of the interior before going into effect.

On March 22, three days after the submission of the petitions, Toby Eagle Bull, secretary of the Oglala Sioux Tribal Council, filed an official request with Superintendent Lyman that the BIA furnish the tribe with an up-to-date list of qualified voters for their use in verifying the signatures and, further, that the fifteen-day period specified for that inspection not begin until after that list was compiled.

The number of eligible voters in the tribe was a crucial issue here. The last referendum election called by the secretary had taken place on October 1, 1969, with the purpose of amending the tribal constitution and bylaws. At that time the BIA had used the figure 3,104 for the number of tribal members entitled to vote. The presenters of the petition also used that number and were certain that their 1,450 signatures constituted well over the required one-third. The elected leadership of the tribe, however, contended that this was not an accurate figure for 1973. For one thing, the voting age had been lowered to eighteen years, which would have increased greatly the number of voters in the tribe from the 1969 figure. The work on the tribal roll and the results of the count are discussed at several points in the superintendent's account.

As the occupation dragged into its fourth week, the attention of the press began to wane. A number of press representatives were withdrawn. ABC radio and television recalled some of its crews who had been maintaining round-the-clock vigils outside Wounded Knee. The *New York Times*, The *Los Angeles Times*, and Reuters News Agency all withdrew reporters. The press corps at news conferences held on March 22 and 23 was much reduced.

With the deadlock in negotiations, violence from within the AIM fortress increased. Forays outside the Wounded Knee perimeter and assaults on federal positions became more numerous and more threatening. There were exchanges of gunfire between the militants and federal emplacements every night, sometimes amounting to between five hundred and one thousand rounds from each side. Under those conditions it was only a matter of time until serious injury would be inflicted. That happened on Sunday, March 25, when Lloyd Grimm, one of the U.S. marshals manning a federal bunker, was critically wounded in the chest by a high-powered rifle bullet. Then, what represented to many on the reservation the ultimate act of violence befell one of their own: that same Sunday, March 25, Leo Wilcox, a member of the tribal council and a friend and staunch supporter of Dick Wilson, was found burned to death in his car on the road to Scenic, a site north of the reservation, near the Badlands National Monument. Although the evidence was lacking, many believed he was murdered by AIM.

Shocked and sickened, the tribal leadership undertook drastic action of its own. More than once in the month-long crisis, Dick Wilson had declared that he was willing to lead an armed force of Sioux volunteers into Wounded Knee to evict the occupiers. He and the tribal council stopped short of that and instead decided to establish their own roadblock on the main route into Wounded Knee, to be manned twenty-four hours a day by armed volunteers. This roadblock was in place Monday morning, March 26, in front of the main government roadblock, with the intention of letting nothing and no one except representatives of the Department of Justice pass into the AIM stronghold. The tribal roadblock, as Lyman referred to it, was to become yet another source of conflict in the remaining weeks of the siege of Wounded Knee.

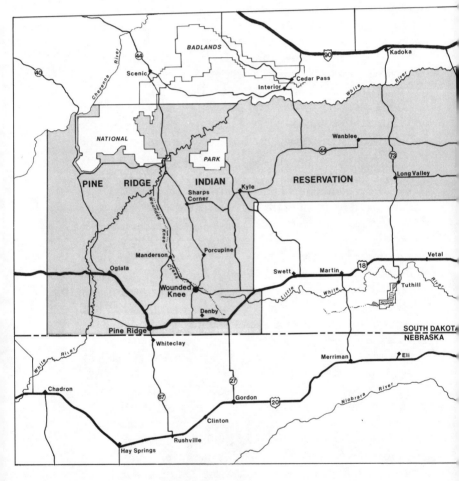

Wounded Knee and environs

The Diary

February 22, 1973

When I looked out my window this morning, the sun was shining, bright and beautiful. Two little guys, little Indian boys, were walking up the street, kicking beer cans and trying to step in mud like kids do, happy, not really aware of what was going on in the adult world around them. I had to say a little prayer that these little folks would not be touched by the events that would occur today.

I got over to the BIA office pretty late. I had had instructions from the federal marshals to stick close to the command post. Of course, they had been taking particular attention with my security, my personal security. A marine bag I carried with me over to the office had my shaving gear, toothbrush, all of my camera gear, and a tape recorder. I thought to myself, "Stan, you might be able to use these today."

From the outside of the building, I could see the sandbags on the roof. I could see the smart-looking, blue-uniformed marshals walking back and forth up there, observing. There were three command posts sandbagged in on the roof. People kept coming by on the street, between the office and the jail, to take a look. One was Judge Hobart Keith, an Oglala Sioux councilman. He carried all of his paint and everything, including his rifle, in the back of his car. He stopped to visit for a while. One of his first remarks when he looked at the marshals was, "They told me, and I didn't believe it!" Another was Gabby Brewer, a little guy, jolly, delightful—a little guy, kind of happy-go-lucky. Yet sticking out of the backseat of his car was a Remington pump rifle—a real beat-up one, but I knew that he could use it. "Gabby," I said, "get that gun out of sight." He said, "Gee, I forgot about it." Dick Colhoff, special officer in charge of the BIA police on the reservation, came by and visited a bit, then Dick Little, Oglala Sioux councilman.

Dick Little and I talked about what he was going to do in the upcoming meeting of the tribal council. Dick was determined to get the council meeting moved to the open floor of Billy Mills Hall rather than in a closed session in the regular room downstairs.

The warehouse over by the jail was full of blue-uniformed officers. Roads employees were busy pulling cars out of the way so that if our friends from AIM, the American Indian Movement, did show up, they would not be able to use them as firebombs. I went up into the office, which was completely different from what it used to be just a couple of days before. There was no one around except uniformed officers and federal marshals. I went into the command post, which was set up in the Roads office, in the south wing. Across the hall, in Land Operations, was the regional director of the FBI. He was sitting off in one corner in a little office set up for him there. In the Roads office, along with the command post, were the U.S. attorney for South Dakota, William Clayton, and a dozen or so FBI people. There was an elaborate radio and communication post set up, with all kinds of radios and telephones and control panels. One big officer was sitting there, typing out everything that happened and phoning it in, every hour on the hour, to the director of marshals in Washington, D.C. I could see rifles, just one or two, lying around. One of them was a very fine sniper rifle—small-caliber, fast, with a flat trajectory—a Remington 25-06. Everybody had a gas mask, and incidentally, you don't feel very comfortable when you find out that all of the gas masks have been issued out and that you are the *only one* in the building without one!

Evidently, if grenades were to be used from here, they would be fired from shotguns, because the shotguns and the gas grenades were all laid out, ready to fire. A big fan was set up in front of the window to blow the gas back away from the building, should gas be used. The window had already been taken out to form a lookout post. The air-conditioning was a big worry since if we had to fire any gas it would all be drawn back in through the intake system. We had to hunt up Pryor, the building manager, to have the system shut off.

On a tour around the place I spoke with U.S. Marshal Reese Kash, who told me that AIM was definitely coming today. I questioned him about his source, as to whether or not it was reliable. He made a curious remark, something to the effect that "Well, I can't tell you that it is from wiretapping because that is illegal. Let me just say that it is from a very reliable source." Naturally, this made me wonder how the FBI and the U.S. Marshal Service manage to get some of the information they get. They, of course, would not reveal this, but they *must* have wiretaps and they *must* have undercover people because otherwise there would be no way of knowing some of the things they know. Of course, AIM is doing the same to us. I don't know whether or not the FBI could be directly infiltrated by AIM, but the BIA certainly is.

I stayed around the command post for a while, as I had been told to do by the chief of security. I heard all of the communications which entered and left the command post, like reports from Rapid City telling exactly where the AIM people were. People at our command post could know this within an hour or two at any time of day—if they wanted to, that is. During the day, information reached us that about seventy-five to a hundred hard-core AIM individuals were sitting around talking at the Mother Butler Center in Rapid City, apparently ready to move in on Pine Ridge at a call from their friends. We don't know what would bring about that call, and of course, I feel that if the call never comes, and if those outside people stay away, this problem can and will be handled locally.

I was getting pretty tired of sitting around that command post, so I told the security people that I was going over to the Oglala Sioux council meeting. Of course they wanted to send a couple of marshals with me, and I declined. I could not put myself under the care of a guard in a situation like that, so I went over by myself. The council was already in session when I got there, and all twenty members of the council were in attendance. Most amazing! Only one time previously, on the occasion of another AIM intrusion, had all twenty members been present. The motion to get the council held in open session had been successful, and the council was meeting, as Dick Little had insisted, in Billy Mills Hall. Not more than seven hundred people were in attendance, which surprised me. I had previously estimated that about fifteen hundred would have been there.

One of the big points of contention at the meeting was the peaceful demonstration of the Oglala Sioux Civil Rights Organization, a group which, as far as we can tell, is sponsored by AIM. They had come into town this morning, right on schedule, perfectly peaceful, but with some fairly inflammatory signs—not really inflammatory, I guess, just critical. One of the signs was quite clever; it said, "Lyman, we don't want your Dick," meaning Tribal Chairman, or President, Dick Wilson. The stage was set for the showdown between the supporters of President Wilson and the anti-Wilson forces looking to have him impeached. The Wilson opponents were led by Dave Long, vice president of the Oglala Sioux Tribe. They have accused Wilson of such things as nepotism, corruption, misuse of tribal funds, false arrest of Indian dissenters on the reservation, protecting bootleggers, and hiring what they call a "goon squad" to enforce his authority. In council, the Wilson forces were sitting at one end of the room and the impeachment forces were sitting at the other. A few members of the Long forces were waving their signs a bit, but I didn't get to read them.

The council proceeded in a very subdued fashion, which was amazing. Even volatile types like Hobart Keith were subdued. Interestingly enough, Dick Wilson seemed to want to get it over with. The immediate issue was whether to accept the charges against Wilson and to proceed with impeachment at once, or to accept the charges and then wait twenty days for the impeachment trial. The opposition forces wanted to wait the twenty days. I don't know what their tactic was in wanting to wait, but they might have figured that they would have Toby Eagle Bull, current secretary of the Oglala Sioux Tribe, as president during that time. I think that they wanted to bypass Dave Long and get Toby Eagle Bull to be president. At least, this was what Hobart Keith told me his strategy would be.

There developed quite a floor fight over how this question was to be handled. Finally the council voted to accept the charges and to hear them immediately. This meant that Wilson had waived his twenty-day right to prepare, and it also put the complainants in a poor position, because now they did not have time to prepare either. Evidently, they had not prepared their case beforehand. Otherwise it is hard to see why they were disturbed about the case being settled at this particular session rather than after a twenty-day period. I have wondered what their objective was.

The rest of the day was taken up deciding who was to be the judge, or presiding officer, of the impeachment council. At one point even I was considered! After considering many names, they finally selected Vincent Thunder Bull. The only thing Vincent Thunder Bull did was to maneuver the council into a recess until tomorrow morning, February 23. A few outside AIM activists, from Minnesota, came in just about the time everybody was leaving the hall. For a time it looked as if a fight might develop, but none did.

I personally felt really good about being back in Billy Mills Hall with the council in session. This was the place I belonged. This was my job. I could feel the admiration and respect and liking of many of them, and I could also feel the hate coming from many others.

Back at the command post, we got word that AIM was not coming tonight because they had not yet received the message to come. They may come to Pine Ridge tomorrow, though. This further supports everyone's conjecture that AIM is waiting for a call from Pine Ridge. I called my bosses at the BIA area office in Aberdeen and had my signal check with the security people. I went home rather let-down because nothing happened today when I was keyed-up and ready for it. At the same time, I was damned glad that nothing did happen because I sure don't want anyone to get hurt in this deal. So the little boys from this morning, wherever they are now, were untouched by the incidents of the day.

February 23, 1973

A busy day: long, hectic, and worrisome. First off, I had visitors at home. Sergeant-at-Arms Brown and his wife came to my home, escorted by Marshal Kash. For the first time, I realized that he was one of the Sioux who had visited me in Utah back in 1971. This morning he had complaints about BIA employees, people who, he said, "felt that they owned the records" and "paid no attention to the Indians." He wanted land-sale money but was unable to get it, the office being closed because of the activities of the day.

Over in town the law was all over the place. Town was full of cars. The marshals had taken down their sandbagged command posts from the roof of the agency building and laid the sandbags out flat on the roof so they were not visible—"keeping a low profile," as they called it. That's where the bags should have been yesterday as well. They probably should have left them on the roof, out of sight, ready to be thrown into a defensive parapet if need be, rather than display them defensively, as they did.

The council meeting began. Sergeant-at-Arms Brown was there and not more than 150 others, at least at the beginning. The council folks were in a circle out in the middle of Billy Mills Hall. There was only a loudspeaker system this time, and the television cameras were gone. For the greater part of an hour, there was hassling over points of procedure and so forth. It was the first time I had ever seen Dick Wilson wearing a suit. He looked good. He seldom wears a pants-and-jacket combination.

Sly innuendos were made by Hobart Keith about Dick Wilson's activities in Denver. The maneuver of the complainants, as I've said, was to get a twenty-day delay period before the charges were heard. Obviously, they did not have their case ready. There were also maneuvers by Dick Little and others to keep Bat Richards from representing Dick Wilson. The issue finally came down to the fact that they were depriving Wilson of a legal defense under the 1968 Civil Rights Act. The ordinance which said that he could *not* have defense counsel dated back to 1941. Dick Wilson finally said that he would represent himself. By then there were about three hundred people present in the hall, and there was clapping whenever the complainants would make a point. Finally the presiding officer, Vince Thunder Bull, said, "Okay, any more clapping and we will go into executive session."

In the meantime, Nick Crazy Thunder came over to me and said that the employment-assistance checks were not out and folks were looking for them. Lloyd Eagle Bull, the employment-assistance officer, had been told to get those checks out to the people, and there he was, sitting in the council hall. I called him over and found that he knew that the checks were there, locked in the safe, and he was not doing anything about it. I had to leave the council to get that taken care of. I went over to the office and got Lloyd Eagle Bull into the vault and got the checks out and made arrangements to see to it that he distributed them. He didn't like it very well. I wish I could describe this attitude, prevalent in the bureaucracy, of not following through, of not taking the initiative. Terrible!

I was away from the council for a while, and by the time I finished, it was the noon recess. I didn't get any lunch at the recess; I was making calls— checking, seeing what was going on, keeping people informed, getting information. The radio was crackling; the telephone was ringing; then a few minutes of quiet without either of these in my own office or in the command post.

The council session resumed at one-thirty, but I was ten minutes late getting back to it. I was waylaid outside the hall by Tony Whirlwind Horse. Tony is the assistant super-intendent for education on Pine Ridge, a beautiful all-Indian guy, good-looking today in his yellow jacket. He was calm and composed, but there was urgency in what he said: "The efforts of the complainants have not gone well, so Dick Wilson is going to be taken on the floor, kidnapped." About that time Nick Crazy Thunder came up, just as urgent. "They have got to have you in the council hall," he told me. "They are calling for you."

Possible kidnapping takes precedence over anything else, so I gave the command post a call. I told them to be sure to let Tony Whirlwind Horse in so he could report the details to Marshal Kash. Marshal Kash had left temporarily on other business, so I had to get the information to the top marshal on the scene. I had to notify Del Eastman as well. Del is in charge of our BIA police, and he was also the one in charge of the Billy Mills Hall scene. Since this was where the kid-napping might take place, I had to take the time to inform him too.

I entered the council and was invited up to a place of promi-nence just outside the council ring, along with Frank Fools Crow, Jim Red Cloud, and Ellis Chips, respected men steeped in the old traditions. Rather than take a place in the coun-cil like that, I pulled my chair back just a little, not wanting to presume. I refused to put myself in a station with the re-vered men of the Oglala Sioux Tribe. Besides, let's face it, I was scared.

Almost immediately I was approached by Birgil Kills Straight, who looks about as AIM as anybody can. He doesn't trust me, as I was soon to find out, but he squatted be-side me and said, "I need duplicate copies of my papers. The judge has called for them as evidence, and these are the only ones I have. So please, can I get them duplicated in your office?" I left the room, and Birgil Kills Straight and Dick Little followed me out. Dick Little was mad at me because I had not been in the council earlier, and told me so.

The three of us went over to the office. The marshals

were shocked at the entry of two obviously AIM types, but I assured them that these were respected councilmen. The councilmen got busy and searched out a duplicator. I was uneasy about it because I knew that Dick Wilson sure as hell would be mad if he knew that I was doing this. Nevertheless, I do have to provide any service that can be offered to either side in this issue. Certainly, they could not give their only copies of these documents to Judge Thunder Bull.

After many false starts with the machine, we finally got it going; one of the marshals showed us how. It was here that I found out that Kills Straight doesn't trust me. He wouldn't let me see what was being duplicated. I insisted on only one copy each. I got some attention from the head marshal in the building, who asked if the councilmen were coming upstairs. I told him no. Little and Kills Straight finally got their documents copied, accompanied with comments from Kills Straight like "Hey, you know, we are really going to get him on this one" and "Boy, this is the one that will kill him" and so forth.

Afterward I started back to the council, but I didn't quite get there because the thing was breaking up and the crowd was streaming out into the parking lot. I walked past one fellow who looked like he was either drunk or else had been drunk all of his life. Probably a little of both. He said to me, "*You* did it to us, *ennit?*"—which means "is that not so?" As he walked away he said, "I will kill you." Del Eastman, who was standing a few yards away, came over, and I told him what the fellow had said and that he looked a little bit drunk. "Maybe you might want to check it out," I said.

I went on to the council hall. The session was all broken up. The only guy around was Toby Eagle Bull, the secretary of the tribe. I asked him, "Toby, what's going on? What do we need to do now?" He said, "Well, watch. There may be trouble." About that time one of the policemen from the neighboring Rosebud Reservation came over—a big, tall, good-looking guy. He said, "Chairman Wilson is in your office and wants to see you." I started back to the office thinking, "Well, the

son of a bitch! Now that he has won he is going to start clean-
ing house, and the first thing that he is going to do is clean
out the superintendent!" I also started wondering what the
hell I was going to say to the bastards. Two policemen fell in
behind me and stayed right with me all the way over.

When I got to the office, I found an entirely different situation from what I had expected. The two guards and I were let
into the BIA building, as usual, by the marshals. They were
all in a state of alert, getting their helmets on and getting
ready to go out. I found no one in my office, so we went on
upstairs to the command post. There, in the old Land Operations room where the FBI had been, were Chairman Dick
Wilson and all of his family. They had been placed in protective custody by the marshals. So instead of a violent, terrible,
vindictive Dick Wilson, ready to fire me, I found a very subdued Dick Wilson with his family around him.

What had happened was that while I was gone from the
council to take care of the duplicating, the group opposing
the president had walked out of the council! I learned that I
had inadvertently led the group away when Dick Little and
Birgil Kills Straight followed me out of the hall. Boom—that
was the end of the opposition, and all the rest of the folks
against the president got up and walked out. I guess that's
what the guy meant who threatened me outside the hall.
With five members gone, the council voted fourteen, with
one abstaining, to accede to the wishes and the threats of
Hobart Keith to get the matter into federal court. The fifteen
remaining councilmembers also passed two resolutions: One
was that they would ask the FBI for a complete investigation
of tribal finances. The other was that they would ask the U.S.
attorney to investigate subversive activity on the Pine Ridge
Reservation.

Then there was an intense period in which Russell Means
—braids and all, but very subdued in appearance this time—
was apparently trying to intimidate the council. Means is a
local Oglala and is a major leader in AIM both locally and
nationally. He was trying to get the two representatives from

his home district of Porcupine—Orlando Big Owl and Bill High Hawk—to walk out of the session, as some of the others had already done. This confrontation lasted several minutes, but the two representatives would not leave. Means himself walked out, and everything broke up. The police stepped in and escorted Dick Wilson and his family from the council meeting. The police did an excellent job in getting them safely out of the hall and into the BIA building.

No one knew what would happen next, but suddenly we were getting ready to put on gas masks. Dick Wilson was a little bit proud. He was shaky. As I said, it was a very, very subdued Dick Wilson who met me at the command post. His family was in jeopardy, and his own life had been threatened, as had the lives of many others.

Pretty soon I decided I had better call my boss, Al Dubray, at the BIA area office and tell him what was going on. In the background was the clunk, clunk, clunk of the sandbags being put back up as parapets on the roof. That dull, rhythmic sound is one of the things I will always remember. I surely wished that I were sitting up there in the area office instead of here facing all of this. What I wanted to tell Dubray was the result of the council vote, but as we were talking Mike Windham, BIA area special officer, who was sitting there with me, interrupted, saying, "Okay, people are coming!" I looked out and sure enough, there were a whole bunch of them across the street, and they were heading right for the front end of either the tribal building or the BIA building. It was quite a sight: a hundred folks walking along there. I told the boss that I had a group of people coming and that I was going to check it out.

I went up the hall and looked again, and sure enough, there they were, all standing in front of the BIA building, right on the sidewalk, right close up. At the time I didn't know it, but some were yelling, "Shoot him!" This was referring to the marshals who were on the roof. One marshal was hit by a slingshot pellet, but that was the only casualty so far.

There were friends in the crowd, like Jo Cornelius, our

secretary, and her brother Roger. I knew that they were not part of a destructive force, but anyway, they were right there in front! There were a few others that I knew were not destructive either. The former law-enforcement committeeman Oscar Hollow Horn was there. I saw a few others that I knew. I can't remember all of their names. Looking out over the group, the marshals could tell that some of those folks were armed. As it turned out, there must have been about twenty-five or thirty people in that group of one hundred who were determined to make a play. Head Marshal Reese Kash, calm and cool, went out and talked to them. He joked with them and talked them out of it but had to listen to a speech from Hobart Keith in the process. Hobart Keith is very eloquent, widely read—can quote poetry and cite history to fit any occasion. There is nothing like a speech from Hobart Keith!

Inside it was very tense. The next thing we knew, everybody got a gas mask. It was quite a sight to see Dick Wilson's family sitting there with a whole stack of gas masks in front of them, trying to put them on. I put mine on and couldn't breathe in it, so I figured that I would just have to go without any protection if they did start using gas. The marshals were ready, of course. They were standing up there at the window ready to take whatever defensive action was necessary. It took quite a while for the tension to die down. In fact, it never did die completely.

Later we had a visit from the Oglala Sioux Civil Rights Organization. There were five representatives of this group out there, and I was going to tell them that I would talk to any two of them. In the meantime, Marshal Kash saw them before I could get that message to them and went out and talked them into going back to Calico Hall, the center of the opposition to the current tribal government. Next we had a visit from White Wolf and Torrance of the Community Relations Service Division of the Department of Justice. They had heard that the council had passed a measure today restraining all outside Indians from coming on the reservation. I checked on that with Toby Eagle Bull and was told that it wasn't true. I told the two guys from Justice that no such measure had been passed, but they still didn't believe it. By then it was five o'clock. A whistle sounded loud in the still, calm air around Pine Ridge.

Much later, things were calming down. Around seven, maybe eight o'clock, I decided to try on that gas mask again and found that it really did work. Training going back thirty years came back to me, along with a little quick instruction from the marshals. I was going to test for five minutes, but after about two minutes my boss called and I had to take it off. I talked with him, and then I ran the test over again, a full five minutes this time. I found that all I had to do was just breathe normally, not gulp, and not move around too fast.

About this time I finally got a chance to eat: an apple and a cookie and a half-pint of milk, the first I had had since morning. That and some potato chips was all I got for the whole day.

Dick Wilson's family was finally escorted off the reservation by the BIA policemen. The chairman himself was told to stay at the post, meaning in the BIA building, and so he did. I phoned over to Nebraska and got the policemen over there to shut down the bars. I ended up talking to the state attorney from Rushville, which is in Sheridan County, Nebraska.

After a while the tension eased. Dick Wilson, Leo Wilcox, and I were sitting in Quentin Sulze's office talking [Sulze was a member of Lyman's staff]. Leo Wilcox told of experiences up on Mount Rushmore and on the top of Sheep Mountain. What he talked about was weird. He referred to four, a sacred Sioux number. There does not seem to be much logic in what he said, but here are some snatches of it.

At Sheep Mountain, four individuals—Sievert Young Bear, and three others I don't remember—were going through their vigil, and a snake came out and crawled by one of them. Somehow Leo interpreted this as being a threat by AIM. He said that this was significant because there were four people who had struck at Chairman Dick Wilson.

Then Leo told of walking around on Mount Rushmore and falling and how a big man came to pick him up. When he fell, Leo was right close to the tops of the faces of the U.S. presidents, and it is very dangerous to get around up there. A big man came to help him get up, but the man never touched him. He just stood there in front of Leo, and through a kind of spiritual help, Leo was able to get up and go on. The people down below saw Leo and the big man walk out on the top of Jefferson's head and saw them walk away and then disappear right in plain sight.

Leo also told of walking with the rangers of Mount Rushmore park—not among them, exactly, just right close by them and invisible to them. They were looking right at him and could not see him. He also told of walking among the group who were followers of Lehman Brightman and told what a cold shoulder he got from them. Anyway, he felt that these four incidents pointed toward the trouble we are having now at Pine Ridge.

As I mentioned before, the marshals have a pretty good intelligence network and so does the FBI. I have wondered where this comes from, because their information generally appears to be quite accurate. One of the messages that came through tonight was that AIM had decided that they were going to kill themselves a marshal. The marshals had men patrolling the roof, and when this information came in they immediately put on flak vests. They came in to where Dick and I and Leo were sitting and saw Dick sitting next to the window. They told him to get away from that window and to sit where he could not be seen. One of the marshals, in great anger, was putting on his flak vest to go out and stand on the roof, knowing full well that a flak vest would not stop a high-powered rifle. He said, "Would you believe that we have difficulty getting overtime pay?"

I decided to go home. My wife, June, had left earlier to drive over to Chadron College in Nebraska to stay at the girls' dormitory there. When I left the house this morning I wasn't too sure that she would go. When things started heating up I asked my secretary, Jo, to check around, and she found that June had in fact gone to Chadron. The marshals felt really good that she was out of there.

I walked over to the house with Leo. We were going to sit down and have a drink, but Leo called his house, and when he got a busy signal he rushed out and went home. I had been told to stay in the BIA building along with Dick. I guess I decided that I have been in this business too long to be hiding overnight behind guards. Besides, the bed over here at home is a hell of a lot more comfortable, so I came home. Nothing happened all night except a call from that redheaded woman of mine. She was telling about the wonderful time she was having at the girls' dormitory in Chadron. "Just like old times," she said.

March 27, 1973

The occupation of Wounded Knee is one month old today. It took place not on February 22 or 23, as we had thought it would, but on February 27. I have been off duty for the past two days, which gives me only fifty or sixty off-duty hours so far in March. In February I was off duty only twenty-nine hours in the entire month. The pressure has been enormous. I have had to maintain my composure at all times. Still, the situation for me personally is appreciably different now from what it was a month ago. Then I was directly involved in making decisions which related to whether or not people were going to get killed. For the last month I have not been personally involved in most of the decisions which could result in death. This has made it somewhat easier for me, but harder for others.

Since the takeover of Wounded Knee was a violation of federal law, the Justice Department of the United States has moved into the situation, and they are calling the shots in terms of negotiations and, in fact, anything that goes on. This flows naturally from the normal relationship which links an

Indian tribe, the BIA, and the Justice Department. In case of a violation of a federal law by an individual, the BIA immediately steps out of it, and the FBI, in the name of the Justice Department, takes over. The situation here is similar except that there are at least a couple of hundred people who have violated federal law. It is a little different when you are dealing with two hundred instead of one.

The federal agencies represented here are many. The FBI, of course, is charged with gathering evidence on crimes that are committed: they call it case building. The U.S. Marshal Service is charged with the duty of protecting federal buildings and enforcing federal law generally. The Community Relations Service within the Justice Department has the job of maintaining liaison between opposing forces in situations of confrontation. Our BIA area director, Wyman Babby, thought we ought to have our own public relations officer, and he is to be complimented for this. So we now have two individuals loaned to us from the Department of Interior. One of them is Jim Harpster, who is ordinarily public relations officer at Denver for the Bureau of Reclamation. The Department of Interior is represented by me and occasionally by Wyman Babby, but we are not listened to very much. The assistant to the secretary of the interior for Indian affairs, Marvin Franklin, was here for a very short time, and we have a lawyer from the Department of Interior present at all times. Right now the Department of Interior lawyer is Hans Walker, from the Fort Berthold Reservation. He comes from a fine Indian family in western North Dakota and is normally head of the Water Rights Division in the BIA Central Office. He seems to be listened to more than the rest of us, with the exception, of course, of Assistant Secretary Franklin.

The Justice Department has been represented by Harlington Wood, who is assistant U.S. attorney general, Civil Division. He is a great man and very astute. Dick Hellstern is here also, the deputy assistant U.S. attorney general. He is a youngster compared to Wood, but nevertheless is a pretty good lawyer—a little bit worried about making decisions.

Another was Charles David Ablard, associate deputy attorney general. Ablard was the one who blew the first negotiations with AIM. These Justice Department representatives are constantly in touch on these matters with Attorney General Richard G. Kleindienst. They are in touch quite a bit with the White House as well. At this particular time, the White House seems to be calling the shots. As of right now, the fellow in charge of Justice Department operations is Kent Frizzell, who is the assistant U.S. attorney general, Land and Resources Division. He is the nominee for head solicitor for the Department of Interior and is a real smooth guy. The Justice Department also has their own public relations officers.

One of the things we have noticed about the way the Justice Department handles this matter is that they appear to deal with Indians as the BIA must have done twenty-five or thirty years ago. I am referring now to the fact that they do not consult at all with Indian tribes and with elected Indian leadership. They make decisions which directly affect Indian leadership through discussions with Kleindienst and possibly the White House. Then they rush out and try to get hold of the "chief," as they call him, tell him about what they have already decided, and try to get him in on their side. This sounds to me like the way the BIA used to do business. Generally, the BIA does not do this anymore, but we are still accused of it.

One of the really significant things about this whole situation is that this is the first time AIM and its national leadership have directly challenged tribal government. The takeover at Wounded Knee came largely through the efforts of what appears to be an AIM-sponsored organization known as the Oglala Sioux Civil Rights Organization. This group is composed of individuals who were disgruntled because of the failed effort to impeach Tribal President Dick Wilson in council last February 23. In the wake of that failure, AIM called for the resignation of Wilson and the dissolution of the Oglala Sioux tribal government. Now, whether the tribal president is corrupt or not, as they say he is, is rather beside the issue. This is a matter of revolution! One month ago tonight, a group of armed individuals, mostly from other tribes but with a few local Indians, occupied and ransacked the Wounded Knee trading post, destroyed the post office, destroyed a very fine museum there, and held around ten or eleven people hostage. They shot at BIA fire trucks that were coming in, and our BIA fire-control people pretty nearly got killed. They also shot at the FBI, at BIA police, and at federal marshals who were moving into the area. They set up roadblocks and would not let anyone in opposition to them come into the area. When postal inspectors came to investigate, they were arrested and paraded before news cameras; then their money, guns, and credentials were seized, and they were sent out of the area with their hands behind their heads. The occupying force out there has proclaimed an "independent state" at Wounded Knee. In any other nation this would be called revolution. I haven't figured out yet what they call it here!

The AIM leadership here appears to be composed of the following: Russell Means, Dennis Banks, Vernon Bellecourt, Clyde Bellecourt, Carter Camp, and Pedro Bissonette. Means is a local Oglala who is in competition with Dick Wilson and who would like to be tribal president. Bissonette is a local Oglala too, who is out on bond after running down a federal officer. The officer was attempting to arrest him on a warrant issued on the basis that he had assaulted a State of South Dakota employee with a deadly weapon.

This past month the marshals, the FBI, and the BIA have maintained seven different roadblocks around Wounded Knee, and there has been a kind of halfhearted effort to seal the area off. The press keeps making a big thing about it, though, and so do the lawyers, so the seal-off has not been very effective. As of the moment, maybe half of the residents of Wounded Knee have left; their homes have been taken over by AIM individuals. There seem to be maybe 100 or 150 hostile (if I may use the word) Indians, who are in the area and who are determined to die. Of course, the impression of some of us is that what they would really like is to have some sixteen-year-old pregnant Indian gal die, and that would give them a martyr.

Quite a variety of individuals not directly involved in the takeover have been on the scene at one point or another. Angela Davis was here and was run off by the tribal police. Also here was Hank Adams, who was the chief negotiator for AIM in their takeover of the BIA building in Washington last fall. He was run off, again by tribal police, and was served with a court order to get off the reservation. Rev. John Adams has been here with about twenty-five members of the National Council of Churches. They were run off, but the reverend is still here. Numerous hippie types were run off. Numerous pressmen were excluded because they had press connections with underground papers. All this was done on an order of the Oglala Sioux Tribal Court based on their constitution and on the decision of the tribal council meeting. Their directives are enforced by a federal agency, the BIA police, which is directed locally by the BIA superintendent. This is roughly comparable to the FBI enforcing orders of the Court of the State of South Dakota.

There have been several people wounded in the confrontation so far. A young man from AIM blew his hand off the first night. Another one was shot in the leg, and a third through the hand. A young Chicano whom the AIM people called a medic volunteer had a scratch on him like a good barbed wire scratch. The latter three of these elected to remain within the AIM perimeter. One FBI agent, Curtis Fitzgerald, was shot in the left hand and in the right forearm and pretty nearly bled to death, but he will be okay. A couple of days ago a federal marshal named Lloyd Grimm, from Omaha, Nebraska, was shot through the chest. The last report on him is that he will never be able to walk again—at least, the chance of his walking again is very, very slight. As of now a cease-fire has been proclaimed, and the marshals have instructions to fire only if their personal life is greatly endangered. The U.S. district court has issued an order to the FBI, the BIA, and the Justice Department to allow six carloads of food to go in daily to Wounded Knee, along with six lawyers. We, of course, had to comply with that.

The president of the tribe, Dick Wilson, has organized a group of about fifty volunteers, mostly mixed-bloods, who have set up their own roadblock in front of roadblock 1. Roadblock 1 is the one which is authorized to control all coming and going at Wounded Knee. But the tribe won't let anybody get up to that roadblock, including the lawyers, whom we are supposed to let in. In this way the tribe is actually acting in defiance of a federal court order. This is not surprising when you consider how the Justice Department has completely ignored the elected leadership of the tribe all of the way through this thing. Actually, they have been paying more attention to AIM than they have to the elected Oglala leadership.

One of the terrible things that has happened over this past weekend is the death of Leo Wilcox. Leo was a member of Oglala Sioux Tribal Council from this district, from right here at Pine Ridge. He had been a violently outspoken critic of AIM and of what has happened at Wounded Knee. He was burned to death on the Scenic road, between Scenic and Rapid City, off the reservation. It is believed, though this has not been proven by investigation, that he might have been a victim of AIM violence. Leo was quite a guy, and his death shocks all of us. He was forty or fifty years old and had served in the Marine Corps. He had to go to Fort Meade Veterans Hospital recently because he was getting a little bit out of touch with the world. As a young man he had studied to be an Oglala Sioux medicine man, so he was full of mythical sayings and feelings and so on. One of the great pleasures of my being here was to listen to him describe some of the things that had happened to him in his mystical quests. June, my wife, knew Leo and his wife thirty years ago when they were in high school and she was a counselor. His last words to June, several days ago, were "We have got to stop this brother fighting brother."

The death of Leo Wilcox is very significant, not only as a personal loss but officially as well, because it could mean that the Oglala Sioux Tribe no longer has a council. Fourteen councilmembers are necessary to constitute a quorum. Six are against Dick Wilson and against the present administration and will almost certainly not show up. With Leo gone, it may be that they will only be able to get thirteen and thus will never be able to have a quorum of the twenty members who are elected to the council. This could mean the effective dissolution of government by tribal council here until Leo's place is filled. It is doubtful, too, whether there will be an election to fill his place.

March 28, 1973

After what is now more than a month of occupation, I can see this war ending without any pictures or even any descriptions of the battlefield. Besides, it is time I checked on the BIA policemen who are here from other parts of the country. So I set out this morning for a tour of the battlefield. One of the things I wanted to do particularly was to visit the BIA posts and bunkers and get the names of the men there and let them know that we are interested in them.

Moot Nelson and I went to Bob Ecoffey's office, which is located out at the airport and which is the planning center of the Oglala Sioux Tribe. Moot is the assistant superintendent of the Pine Ridge Agency, and Bob is the tribal planning director. We picked up a helicopter flight to go out to the main government control point, which they call Red Arrow. On the way we got a briefing on where the bunkers are and things like that. Del Eastman, in charge of the BIA police, picked us up at Red Arrow and took us around back by jeep.

The first bunker Moot and Del and I visited was at roadblock 3. The marshal in charge there was Chris Hansen from Vermont. The bunker consisted of a hole dug in behind an old overturned car and some sandbags. From there you could look directly down at the Wounded Knee trading post. There was an overturned red trailer truck in the yard just to the south of the store. I don't know what the tactical reason for that would be. About four hundred yards to the south of the store, we could see three or four AIM bunkers which had been dug in the field. There were little patches of snow along them that hadn't melted yet. Right on top of the hill, from where we were looking, was another AIM bunker, a large one. This is the bunker which guards AIM's own roadblock, which is on Highway 18, coming in from the south. Looking with field glasses we could see the two overturned and burned-out cars on the road.

I stepped out of the bunker and walked off to the left, where I could see another very big bunker which has been giving this post, roadblock 3, quite a bit of fire. To the right we could see a tepee by the Manderson and Porcupine roads, with three or four vehicles around it. There was also the Catholic church on the hill—one of the landmarks of Wounded Knee—now with bunkers in front of it, people walking around, and a few vehicles. Luckily, there is a cease-fire in force. Over across, in the background, the housing project was visible, quite a ways away, with at least fifteen vehicles around.

From there we went down a ridge to Apple bunker. It was made of an old armored personnel carrier with a white American star on it, a blue truck to the right, and some overturned vehicles standing around it. Del said they had gotten a bunch of old cars from the junk pile to pull in around here. This is the bunker where Marshal Grimm was shot. From there we had a clear view of the big AIM bunker described above; the Church of God, or what we call the Little Church; the little tepee-shaped church; the Wounded Knee store, or trading post; the crossroads of the Porcupine and Manderson roads; and the Catholic church on the hill, as mentioned above.

Several AIM bunkers were in plain sight too. Across the road which leads out of Wounded Knee towards Porcupine is a very troublesome bunker. It is located about fifty yards up the hill from the bridge, which has been destroyed. Another troublesome bunker is farther to the right, in a field there, just to the north of the telephone or power line which runs west into the Wounded Knee housing project, mentioned above. From this angle we could see more clearly. There were people walking about by the bunkers. The AIM bunker by the destroyed bridge looked very comfortable. We could see a chimney with smoke coming out of it and what looked like three firing ports.

Roadblock 4 was our next stop. It is not really in a very good location. There is a ridge between it and the other bunkers, which obstructs the view, but on the other hand, you can't get hit in there because it obstructs the weapons fire as well. We could see from here how much of the country was burned out: more than half of it, I would guess.

From roadblock 4 we continued up toward Porcupine to roadblock Cobra and its bunker, X-ray. X-ray bunker is the first one so far which has been manned by BIA police: Calvin Red Thunder from Fort Peck, Montana; Felix Dickens from Fort Berthold; Sidney Bailey from Standing Rock; Raymond Noranco from Northern Pueblos, in New Mexico. This was a pretty impressive bunker. It wasn't dug in very much, but it was fortified with sandbags and logs built up around it. There was some plywood with dirt thrown on it for a roof, and a couple of stoves inside made it warm and comfortable. This is the bunker that has been taking some pretty rough fire. Del Eastman said that was because it cuts off the avenue of escape and the supply route from Porcupine to Wounded Knee.

One of the things that made me mad out there was flags at the AIM bunkers flown upside down. From X-ray we could see one such flag on the little bunker north of the Catholic church. There was also a grass fire being blown by the wind and spreading, gradually and slowly, to the north toward Wounded Knee. If there hadn't been a war in progress, our Land Operations people would have come charging out from the agency and would have really worked to put it out, but there we were, just watching it burn.

From X-ray we continued on to roadblock 5 and Zebra

bunker, which looks straight east into Wounded Knee. Zebra is also manned by the BIA: Alex Medicine Horse, Nevada Agency; Melvin Grey Bear, Fort Totten Agency; Joe McCloud, Turtle Mountain. This was a pretty nice little bunker too; it looked like a tepee! It had sandbags built around in a circle, then plywood slanted up into a conical shape, with dirt and pine boughs on top. Looking out, we could tell the war had been going on for quite a while, from the looks of the different burned-out areas. Right in front of us was some stuff that had almost grown back to normal, but a little farther off, the ground was coal-black from recent burning. We also remarked that we now know what happened to the $125,000 worth of lumber and material which belonged to the contractor of the housing project. It's all down there in those bunkers!

It was interesting to compare the FBI roadblocks to those of the BIA and the marshals. The FBI just seemed to set their cars and personnel carriers out on the open ground and then stand there and freeze and gripe about it. The BIA and the marshals, on the other hand, dug in and really did a nice job of making a relatively permanent and comfortable location of it.

The tour of the perimeter took up most of the day, but there were other things that happened, too: a day of conflict all around. First off, we got word that James Abourezk, U.S. senator from South Dakota and head of the Senate Subcommittee for Indian Affairs, and Marvin Franklin, assistant to the secretary of the interior for Indian affairs, were planning to meet today with dissident Indians in Rapid City. This is surprising and potentially very damaging. Last Saturday the National Tribal Chairmen's Association and the National Congress of American Indians had arranged to meet with congressional delegations in Washington on this very day, Wednesday, March 28. So what were Abourezk and Franklin doing traveling to Rapid City to attend a last-minute meeting with a bunch of militant dissidents instead of remaining in Washington to meet with official representatives of the Indian tribes? Very startling and quite revealing about prevailing attitudes.

Abourezk and Franklin flew through Pine Ridge and picked up Wyman Babby, our BIA area director, and the three of them went on together to Rapid City. It seems that Abourezk criticized and berated the BIA all during the flight, and Franklin said absolutely nothing. When they all got off the plane in Rapid City, Abourezk took Franklin off with him and the two of them just ignored Wyman and left him standing there on the sidewalk. Wyman turned around and came right back home.

By the time Wyman got back and called me in the evening, he was very angry, angrier even than he had been at the time, over the way he was treated and over what had supposedly gone on at the meeting. He had gotten word, unofficially, from a contact in Rapid City, that the BIA had apparently lost everything in the agreements reached at the meeting, and so had the Oglala Sioux Tribe. AIM had asked for the removal of three people: Babby himself, Dick Wilson, and me. Abourezk and Franklin had reportedly agreed to that and had also agreed to hold a referendum, regardless of whether or not the procedure was correct. The point that could not be agreed on was that of amnesty for the AIM people at Wounded Knee. Other than that, it appeared from what Wyman had heard that AIM was winning the whole thing.

I got back from my tour of the perimeter around six o'clock or six-thirty. I decided not to go back to the office because there was sure to be something happening there. Instead, I came directly to the house, had a steak, and hoped to get away without any contact for the evening. Of course, there was Wyman's call and several others besides, so it didn't work out that way. In the morning I'll have to find out what really went on in that Rapid City meeting and sort out some of the other matters I received calls on as well. Spring is coming. It's a beautiful evening, and there is a life away from here too, I guess. At least, that's what June says. She seems really discouraged. She was upset to find that my name was again included with those who would have to go.

March 29, 1973

Things were pretty quiet around the command post today. Nobody was doing any shooting out there, but there was still plenty going on—plenty of conflict of a quieter nature. First there was the business of the meeting at Rapid City. What had Abourezk actually done up there? It seems that the AIM leadership at Rapid City was completely disorganized. Ted Means said that he was just talking for himself. Vernon Belle-court said that he was speaking for AIM. This was in direct opposition to Aaron DeSersa's statement that he was the one speaking for AIM. The result was that the meeting just kind of drifted away. Apparently, none of the things that Wyman Babby was worried about were actually considered in nego-tiation. At any rate, Abourezk is supposed to go back and talk to them again at a later date.

Then there was controversy between Kent Frizzell and Dick Wilson. I had received a call at home last night that Frizzell just had to see Wilson, and see him that night. Dick was in Rushville waiting for Frizzell, and Frizzell was stand-ing around the Pine Ridge police station waiting for Dick. As it turned out, they never got together until this morning. What it was about was that Frizzell was trying to get Wil-son to lift his roadblock. He wanted it lifted for three days. During the day, Wilson talked to his own people and to his attorney and decided that he would not lift the tribal road-block but that he would allow certain designated people to pass through: Senator Abourezk; the Reverend John Adams, the negotiator from the National Council of Churches; and Ramon Roubideaux, the chief legal representative for AIM.

When Wilson told Frizzell of this decision, Frizzell accepted it, of course, which was all he could do.

This morning at the briefing, Frizzell proposed the idea— and it is a pretty good one—of adding a civil rights investigator to the group which now includes representatives from the Justice Department, the Community Relations Service, the United States Army, the BIA, of course, and others. As he said later to the news media: "I keep finding that the personal complaints of individuals are overriding the real issues here. It seems reasonable, therefore, to establish a means of hearing these individual complaints." And of course, he is right. Pursuant to this, he opened negotiations with AIM to allow a representative from the Civil Rights Division of the Justice Department to set up a place inside Wounded Knee where those who felt that their civil rights had been violated could come and report it, with the possibility of their complaints being heard later. Frizzell dealt with Dennis Banks on this, who was the negotiator for Wounded Knee, inside of Wounded Knee, and the proposal was accepted. The only change was that instead of using a bus as the place for the hearings, it would be in the ceremonial tepee in the yard of the Church of God, what we call the Little Church. Interestingly enough, AIM has made a real pitch in the last two or three days to say that all the people in Wounded Knee are local Sioux and that they are the ones in control of the situation. However, when it becomes necessary to negotiate anything, like where the civil rights examiner should sit, it is Dennis Banks who is making the decisions!

We will soon have some facts to counter these kinds of statements from AIM. Today we had the Welfare Department identify for us the total number of people who are residents of Wounded Knee and who have been taken out of Wounded Knee. They also were to identify those residents who are still remaining in Wounded Knee. The Red Cross and the Bureau of Indian Affairs Social Services are making plans for if and when the confrontation comes to a close. The purpose of the census is to enable them to move in immediately with the right kind of help. Knowing the actual number of residents now in Wounded Knee is also useful to us and could have a good deal to do with our evaluation of the situation.

The efforts by the Oglala Sioux Tribe and the U.S. government to keep people out of the occupied area are meeting with variable success. There is an FAA order which says that aircraft cannot land in Wounded Knee. There is a similar order of the Oglala Sioux Tribal Court issued by Red Tibbits, a retired BIA special officer who is now one of the tribal judges. It says that all aircraft except government aircraft are prohibited from flying over the Pine Ridge Reservation. Despite these orders, aircraft are seen regularly flying over the area. While I was out yesterday visiting the roadblocks and bunkers, I saw a light plane land just to the south of Wounded Knee. There are rumors that the planes sneaking into Wounded Knee are flown by Canadian bush pilots. One plane that landed the other day was reported to be of foreign, specifically Canadian, registration. In addition to the orders concerning aircraft, the Oglala Sioux tribal government has in effect another order based on their 1868 treaty. This order bars all non-Indians and foreign Indians not only from Wounded Knee itself but from the entire Pine Ridge Reservation.

In the face of all this, NBC has decided to get themselves a helicopter and to fly in there when negotiations begin in Wounded Knee. Jim Harpster, the chief information officer for the government, is just throwing fits over this because he doesn't know how to stop it. I suggested to Harpster that one way to handle it would be to just tell Dick Wilson what NBC was trying to do. In fact, I told Dick myself and suggested that he should contact his attorney. Probably what Dick will do is just ban NBC from the reservation for violating the orders of the tribal court. We will have to see what happens; we may have a little excitement over this tomorrow.

I had an interesting conversation today by phone with a fellow by the name of Michael Schulman, who is executive director of the Young Men and Young Women's Hebrew Association of the greater Miami area. It seems that the newspapers in Miami have presented this thing as if there were all manner of oppression by the federal government—trying to subdue these poor Indians in Wounded Knee. So the high school kids of Miami rushed out and gathered up ten thousand individual pieces of canned goods to be sent up here to the militants in Wounded Knee. Schulman had called before and had talked to our secretary, Jo Cornelius. Pretty, chic, enthusiastic—Jo is really a brilliant secretary and a great asset. She comes from one of the most prominent and successful families in the Oglala Sioux Tribe. Jo had told Mr. Schulman that if he came up here with the food he would not be allowed into Wounded Knee. She suggested that the food be donated to the Felix Cohen Home for the Elderly here on the reservation. On Schulman's follow-up call today, I ended up spending thirty minutes trying to give him a clear picture of the situation here. Finally, by the time we got through, Schulman realized that he had gotten caught in the middle of something pretty complicated. There he was, stuck between the militant Indians and the tribal government, and he wanted a way out. I suggested again the Cohen home, but he couldn't really buy that. He also wanted to talk to AIM leadership, and I directed him to take it up with the marshals or with Kent Frizzell. I gave him the appropriate phone numbers and then I went up and discussed it personally with Frizzell. I got two other good solutions to his dilemma. One was from Wayne Colburn, the director of the U.S. Marshal Service. He suggested that the canned goods be given to the Red Cross and then they could distribute them. The other was from Frizzell himself, which was to allow the food to be brought in and then, after the Wounded Knee confrontation had ended, we would distribute it to all needy Pine Ridge Indians on the reservation.

Well, the next thing that happened was that we got a call from a reporter from the *Miami Herald*. He was very inquisitive about the situation here: were we starving out these militant Indians? The poor guy didn't really want to listen to any facts in the matter; he just wanted to know if the government was starving out the militants. It was very difficult for him to get the idea that there is a tribal government and that they might not necessarily be in agreement with the militant Indians, as their position had been stated in the press. What was amusing was that he was particularly obtuse in not being able to understand that there were three different kinds of proposals to make legitimate use of the canned goods: one was the Cohen home, for the old people; the second was the Red Cross; and the third was to hold the food and give it to all Oglalas after the confrontation. He just couldn't understand this. He also had a great deal of difficulty understanding whether or not the reservation was surrounded by AIM or whether the reservation was surrounded by the government or whether the reservation was surrounded by Oglala Sioux. I think we finally got it across to him that Wounded Knee is a small village within the Pine Ridge Reservation and that access to it was being limited by the federal government *and* by the Oglala Sioux tribal government. Anyway, he will have a few words to say about all this in the *Miami Herald* and I don't know where the ten thousand cans of food will end up.

Speaking of canned goods, today Moot Nelson, the assistant superintendent, stole a case of C-rations and took it out to the tribal roadblock because they are not having very good luck getting food brought to them during the night. They have only the local people around to bring food in during the day. Not to be outdone, of course, I decided that I would have a case of C-rations "stolen" every day to be delivered to the roadblock.

We got a new man from Interior today: Jim Clear, a nice young man, a big, tall lawyer type who has been with the Solicitor's Office in the Department of Interior. I had worked closely with him before, on negotiations for Public Law 671, the Indian Self-Determination Act, which we helped to push through the Supreme Court. Today he said with great pride, "We won that one, didn't we?" He is third in our string of solicitors from the Department of Interior, having been preceded first by Charlie Soller and most recently by Hans Walker. Of the three, Jim Clear and Charlie Soller are both non-Indian, and Hans Walker, of course, is Indian.

The point is that they rotate everybody in and out except the superintendent. I have been involved in this stupid thing from the beginning of February, through March, up to now. I did have a Sunday and a Monday and a Tuesday off. This is when I went to Salt Lake City. I went for two reasons: one was to get my income tax prepared, and the other was to get the hell out of here. I had to fight to get out, and I had to fight to keep from coming back early. The rest of the boys get rotated; I don't, and I am getting tired of it. Of course, Wilson laughs at all of this. He says, "You guys can rotate out and you have somebody to take your place. You yourself can rotate out and leave the agency with Moot. But if I rotate out, you've got Dave Long and we have lost the whole war." Wilson is under a strain; there is no doubt about it.

We had the auditors at work here again today. They came out from the General Accounting Office at the request of Senator Abourezk's office, and they have been here about a week now. One of the things that they have been investigating is the charge that Wilson has been getting kickbacks on contracts. I had a discussion with them today, and from what they have found so far, it might not have been handled real cleanly, but there is certainly no possibility of there having been massive kickbacks and massive giving of contracts to Dick Wilson's friends, as had been charged.

One of the very disturbing things that I noticed today (I have noticed it all along, but it seemed worse today) is the fact that here is our BIA office, full of marshals, full of all kinds of people who are not related to Indian business, and there are just hardly any Indians here. Usually the place is just full of Indians. I don't know whether or not we were serving them well before, but we are certainly not serving them at all now. It is a real tragedy. In the meantime, the Justice Department goes on negotiating.

A newscast from the television today gave a good summary

of the state of negotiations, so I will include it here. It is by Jerry DeShan, of KUDH, Channel 4, from Hastings, Nebraska:

> Prospects for a negotiated settlement had greatly decreased with the collapse of an armed mutiny within the militant ranks. Ramon Roubideaux, an attorney for the AIM forces who seized Wounded Knee in an armed coup thirty days ago, denied there was any dissension among the occupiers. In addition, Frizzell said that he was informed that the Eighth U.S. Circuit Court of Appeals in St. Louis had turned down a government request. The government was seeking to nullify a U.S. district court order allowing AIM attorneys and medical supplies to pass through government lines into Wounded Knee. In its petition, the government had agreed that federal courts do not have the authority to review the Interior Department's supervision of matters involving reservations. Frizzell said the government will continue to bar shipments of food into the village. He denied charges of militant leaders that the government is preventing persons from leaving the settlement.

I will close today's entry with some observations from June. She has her own sources of information, which are different from mine, and her own perspectives on things, which are always excellent.

> *June Lyman*:
> Today our son, Marty, and I went out to the road-block at Wounded Knee. My reason for going was that I wanted to see how far I could get on the Big Foot Trail to Wounded Knee. We got up about two miles off the highway, probably five miles from Wounded Knee. There were fifteen cars there. This was the volunteer squad known as "Dick Wilson's goons." These are men, mainly Oglala Sioux, who

have some obligation to Dick Wilson. Either he has gotten them a job or he is related to them. As one of my friends in the AIM movement said, "Their life depends upon Dick Wilson; therefore, they are out ready to lay their life on the line for Dick Wilson."

I went in our car, which is identifiable as a local car by the 65 on its license plate. Marty went along in his own car, which has a Utah license. We thought this might cause some alarm because they have told all outsiders to stay away. We drove out to the roadblock and, as I said, there were about fifteen cars there and a number of old tires and logs piled across the road. The men had a fire and were drinking coffee. They did not ask us to have coffee with them. They wanted to know what we wanted, and I said that I only wanted to see how far I could get on the road and that it looked like this was it. One of them said, "Yes, this is it." Then I said, "Well, I guess we will turn around and go back," and he answered, "I will appreciate that." He was a young mixed-blood Indian man whom I did not know. He did not recognize me or the car, but apparently recognized the car license as a local number. Marty took quite a few pictures, and then we turned around and started back. When we got back to the sign that told the story of Crazy Horse, we stopped and read that story again. We took some pictures around the sign and along the Big Foot Trail.

As we came back into the Pine Ridge, we looked at the village again—one of the dreariest, saddest, most miserable villages you could ever see on the face of the earth. Gloomy. The roads running down into the village are so bad that you cannot drive a car in. There were little kids running around, oblivious to the whole thing. We took some pictures of the adults. They were dressed

well and warmly—not fashionably, you understand, but they did have the necessities. Somehow,
I had a feeling like I have when I drive through the
saddest villages of Old Mexico, where I am embarrassed to take pictures. But we did take a few
pictures today, like one of the water tower with its
sign reading "Pine Ridge Indian Village." When I
look at Pine Ridge Indian Village, I am angry, I am
very angry, and the reason is that I don't believe
anything that the American Indian Movement is
doing right now is going to help the miserable
situation here, at least not for a while. The other
reason for my anger is that through thirty years, I
don't think the Bureau of Indian Affairs has helped
that miserable village very much either.

I have something to say about the roadblock,
too. I believe that if the tribal roadblock which is
out there right now, the one manned by the Indians known as "Dick Wilson's goons," had been
there from the very beginning of the invasion of
Wounded Knee, there would not have been the
month of misery, trouble, worry, struggle; the marshal who is paralyzed, the other wounded and dead;
the Indian people who are hurt and homeless and
hungry. I do not believe any of this would have happened. I believe that if the local Oglala Sioux volunteer police and the BIA police had gone out there
right from the beginning and put up the roadblock,
without the news and television coverage, without
the publicity that Banks and Means wanted, then
they could have taken care of it, and this mess that
we are involved in would never have developed to
the point where it is today.

Reading a current newspaper leaves one utterly
confused, with no idea of the leadership, the negotiations, the decision making, or what is going to
happen. It seems to me that it is all developing

into a great state of confusion, and it is so needless. This whole incident could have been handled
locally and handled simply. The BIA police are
very well trained and very capable. The direction
could have come right out of the superintendent's
office here, in cooperation with the Oglala Sioux
Tribal Council. Instead, it has become a national
issue and one which is either ridiculous or tragic,
depending on how it affects various people.

Tonight Stan and I are going to the wake for Leo
Wilcox. A large crowd will be there. Leo was a veteran, and there will be a military service. This is a
sad time in the life of people who knew him personally. So along with all of the personal tragedy
and misery, the occupation of Wounded Knee just
seems to go on and on and on.

March 30, 1973

I got over to the office this morning and went to the briefing
meeting, as usual. This time Frizzell, who is always in charge,
thought that it would be a good idea to introduce everyone.
This is the first time, to my knowledge, that this has been
done around here. Here is kind of a short description of the
major participants who were there today. What a wealth of
talent and experience we have in the persons of these men
and their various areas of expertise, all gathered together here
at Pine Ridge.

Bob Fellcamp and Tom Evans: Our new public-information officers, both nice young men. Evans is from Omaha,
from the Department of Interior. Fellcamp comes from the
Justice Department.

Mike Windham: Assistant area special officer from the
BIA, a good man, kind of slow-talking, doesn't say much, not
too pushy.

Colonel Potter: Deputy chief of staff of the Sixth Army. He is completely informal, sometimes looks like a duck hunter on vacation from hunting ducks. He has his desk clean all the time and never seems to be doing anything at all.

Colonel Bill Williamson: He is replacing Colonel Potter. We'll have to see how he works out.

Colonel Joe Baker: He describes himself as an "intelligence type," in completely civilian clothes. He comes from Fort Bragg, North Carolina.

Herb Hoxie: The F B I agent in charge, fortyish, alert, a sensitive man who appears to know his business and to be really capable.

Wayne B. Colburn: Director of the U.S. Marshal Service. He really knows his business, too, in terms of how to put the Marshal Service together. When he sets out to get something done, he pursues it in a more forthright and forceful manner than does Kent Frizzell, for instance, who is his superior in the Justice Department chain of command here.

George Tennyson: U.S. marshal for South Dakota, middle-aged. I've known him for years.

R. D. Hurd: One of the assistant U.S. attorneys for South Dakota. As prosecutor on the scene, he tells the F B I men whether or not they can make a charge. He is the son of a fellow I knew up in Sturgis, South Dakota.

Dick Hellstern: Deputy assistant U.S. attorney general, Civil Division; a nice young man. In normal times he is Harlington Wood's assistant and probably does an excellent job. But here, filling in for Wood or for Frizzell, he doesn't show the latitude of action or thought that those two do. This is probably because he is younger and not fully in charge.

Jim Clear: The departmental solicitor, whom, as I said before, I worked with on the Indian Self-Determination Act. He's a great big guy, a nice-appearing, good young man.

Dave Davis: From the Department of Interior. I believe he is information officer.

Carl Storber: Civil Rights Division. He will be taking civil rights complaints, and I heard today that he has three already. One is against a former policeman who was fired, John Long, a son of the tribal vice president, Dave Long. Another is against a policeman by the name of Fred Two Bulls, who is going to be fired tomorrow. The third, of course, is against Dick Wilson.

Dennis Ickes: A young fellow from the Civil Rights Division, here to take civil rights complaints from the inside. His job out there at the tepee, the ceremonial tepee, as they call it, will be to just sit and listen to folks who claim their civil rights have been violated.

Kent Frizzell: Assistant U.S. attorney general, Land and Resources Division; a nice-looking man in his middle to late forties—kind of gray frizzled-up hair. He can talk oh so smoothly, so beautifully and persuasively; yet always, in the back of my mind, I don't quite trust him. I always have the impression he is playing at two or three games at once.

Today, in the afternoon, was the burial of Leo Wilcox. We gave all BIA employees the time off so that they could attend the services if they wished. I don't know how many did go to the funeral: quite a few were there and quite a few were not; probably more did not go than did.

Leo had lain in state at Billy Mills Hall for a long time, for several days. There was a kind of short ceremony there before he was taken over to Joiner Hall, which is about fifty or seventy-five yards from Billy Mills Hall. Joiner Hall is the Episcopalian church here at Pine Ridge. There were hundreds of people there. The minister remarked during the service that a number of different kinds of people were there in the congregation today, people who did not know each other but who were there because each of them had known Leo.

And the place was a study, indeed it was. There was the minister himself, a big, good-looking Lakota boy. There was a woman whom I knew years ago, many years ago, as presumably the mistress of one of the workers here. She was there alone, now head of the program where she had worked as a clerk in those days. I wonder how long she had known Leo. There weren't too many of the councilmen there—probably four or five out of the twenty. One of them was a pallbearer.

Other influential men around town were pallbearers too. There were the old, old women, full-blood Sioux. There were the middle-aged and older mixed-bloods. There were the poor people, the full-bloods, with shabby shoes and poorly kept clothes. There were others in dresses and suits, worn to perfection. All of these were joined for a time in saying good-bye to Leo.

The services in the church came to a close, and as the casket went down the aisle to move out to the cemetery, I saw Lenore, Leo's wife. I had known her so many years ago, and again fewer years ago. Now she was walking behind him, tall and straight, but ugly with the pain in her face. I had remembered her as a different kind of person entirely than she was at this time.

At the cemetery the dust was blowing a little bit, of course, and the grass was brown. At the golf course right by the cemetery, there must have been twenty people playing golf as Leo was buried. The grave-side ceremony was stopped for a while because Dick Wilson had to go and get an Oglala Sioux flag to give Lenore to put on the casket in memory of Leo. The fellow who blew taps would have been better off with a Christmas horn or a holiday horn. "The Land Was Fairer than Day" was sung in Oglala. Children skipped over the graves. The Pine Ridge hills were beautiful, as they always are, and Wounded Knee was twenty miles away.

I left the cemetery and went back to the office. Some smart aleck in the marshals' office asked me, "How was the funeral?" What a hell of a question that is.

Leo's sister, Geneva Gonzalez, came to the office after the funeral to see R. D. Hurd, one of the assistant U.S. attorneys for South Dakota. She was certain that there had been foul play in Leo's death. I had talked to Hurd previously about this, and he was just as certain that Leo's burning death was an accident, although a strange one. Anyway, he was wondering how he was going to tell Leo's sister this.

Other things happened as well today. There was more smoke over the matter of press coverage of the negotiations.

As I said before, John Danse of NBC was insisting on going into Wounded Knee by helicopter because he and other members of the press had been barred from the negotiations by the Justice Department and the Oglala Sioux Tribe. Jim Harpster had to handle the hassle from our side, and it looked for a while as if he was going to give in. Eventually, however, he and the press came to a compromise that there would be a pool of press representatives allowed in and only silent video-taping—no sound.

There was a little excitement over a parachute drop today. A pilot from Gordon, Nebraska, flew in and flew around awhile and dropped some material. They caught him when he landed back at Gordon. He claimed that he just flew around over Wounded Knee but never dropped anything. In the meantime, Snooper 1, the FBI helicopter, settled down and picked up the parachute drop. So they have it now and they won't tell anyone what is in it.

We find that we are violating a federal court order by having our government cars at the Wilson roadblock. They were put there so that the men at the roadblock could have radio communication. We took them out immediately, and Buford Daniels, the BIA area radio man, gave us some small radios to give to them instead.

A funny thing happened during the afternoon when Mary Sullivan came to visit the office. Mary lives way out in the boondocks, by the village of Oelrichs. She doesn't pay too much attention to what is going on here, and she hasn't been into town for quite a while. The security around the building has been relaxed a little bit, and the marshals and the FBI have arranged to use a side door to go in and out. That door is supposed to be for their use exclusively. As I mentioned before, the FBI and the marshals are strung out all over two of our big rooms upstairs, the Roads office and the Land Operations office. They don't want anybody at all in these rooms or looking around up there. The FBI is especially fussy about this.

Well, Mary Sullivan had a problem with prairie dogs on her

land and she wanted to get rid of them. She knew that the way to get this done was to talk to the people in Land Operations. So in she walked and up the stairs, with nobody watching her, and went right into the Land Operations office. Suddenly she was surrounded by FBI men, and they really hustled her out of there in a hurry. She said, "I didn't know that everybody was so uptight. All I wanted was to get my prairie dogs killed!" and then she laughed.

When I left the office in the afternoon, I went to Chadron to get the Oldsmobile tuned up. Then I went out to dinner with June and Marty and had a pleasant visit. We went to Herman's, the German place. It is nice to have such a nice place around here and to get out on a Friday night, for a change.

March 31, 1973

Saturday. Not too much work. Strange. It feels like it does on Sunday around here. I did get a phone call in the middle of the night. Wayne Colburn, head of the U.S. Marshal Service, had supposedly run a load of food through Dick Wilson's roadblock. Bessie Cornelius, Jo's mother, called me up last night, cussing and shouting that she was ready to get her bunch of Oglala women out there and stand them in front of those marshals and then just see if they would threaten to shoot women!

There was also a new development in the press-coverage deal. It turns out that Jim Harpster made the agreement with the press representatives all by himself, without consulting tribal officials. Dick Wilson was not even informed of it until after the fact. So today Tom Evans, one of the new information officers, running front for Harpster, who is about to leave, went to ask Dick for permission to do this. Dick Wilson said no, and the negotiators were in the same old trap: they had made their deal and went to sell it to the Indians.

This time the Indians said no, and so the negotiators will have to go back and work out something else.

It is the middle of the afternoon, around five-thirty or so, and up to now I have had exactly one phone call on business. That was from Del Eastman, who was just reporting in to the effect that he was going to take his family and go to Rapid City because things are fairly quiet right now. He had some interesting things to tell. The other night the FBI, the marshals, and the BIA police under Del moved the roadblocks down closer to Wounded Knee to tighten things up. The poor AIM people just screamed something awful: This was a foul; this was a low blow! My goodness, to have this happen in a situation of close fire! So the marshals said they would pull their blocks back. Del tried to leave his there for a while, and he did, but he ended up having to take it back too. He was kind of mad about having to do this. He thinks we need to tighten up our perimeters quite a bit. If they keep letting people come in with food and ammunition, this thing is going to go on all summer.

In the meantime, the Justice Department just plays around at negotiating. Right now all the talking they are doing is nothing but play—no question about it. AIM changes its negotiating position every time they meet or every time things get to the point where there can be an arrangement. The one thing the AIM negotiators cannot accept is for the occupiers of Wounded Knee to agree to come out of there and submit to arrest.

One of the really interesting things Del told me was about the capture of a fellow named Tapio. It sounds like a local name. This Tapio went in as one of eighteen or twenty people who walked into Wounded Knee with backpacks full of ammunition. What they found on him included .22- and .30-caliber ammunition and, I believe Del said, 30.06 ammunition as well. Anyway, the marshals arrested him, and there were about eighteen or nineteen others they didn't get.

One thing that we have become aware of is that the FBI is

watching very closely for AIM people and others who start out from other places in the country with the intention of coming here. I don't know how the FBI infiltrates such groups or how they get their information, but they know who these people are, how many of them are coming, what they are bringing with them. If there is what they call probable cause for a search, then they bust them when they find their fire-bombs and guns and gasoline-bomb-making equipment. This approach is really keeping quite a few people away from here.

Evidently, the FBI has ways of classifying its types of information. Some of it they rely on greatly; other types they don't rely on as much; and others they just classify as rumor. They are presently aware that the next places that AIM is going to hit are very likely to be Hennepin, in Oklahoma, and Gallup, New Mexico.

I found out today that they have identified the man who shot Marshal Grimm. He is a white man named Al Cooper, "Crazy Al," a real radical. Apparently this guy is too crazy even for AIM. Making this identification is pretty impressive when you consider that he was down in a group with a bunch of other people who were all shooting up at the government bunker. They would have to be pretty good to do this; as a matter of fact, I still don't see how they could have done it. Obviously, they have some informant in there, and of course they don't say too much about this. They do know that what they have there is dynamite. A couple of days ago Del Eastman got some special radios, and he fiddled around with them until he got on their code—the wavelength the occupiers are using down there. So now Del is listening to them talk back and forth, just as they have been listening to us for quite a few days.

The first of the week, I am going to try to move the agency out to the various districts to try to carry on some normal business. I will see how that works. It will be hell to get it done, and maybe I can't get it done, but it's time we did something. There is nobody coming into the office now with those guns looking down their throats. Maybe this is a good way for the Bureau of Indian Affairs to go out of business. How about that?

April 1, 1973

This is one of the quietest days we have had in a long time, so June and I took the afternoon off and took a little trip out into the Wakpamani district. This is out east of the Herd Camp Dam and east of where Johnson Holy Rock has his range. When we got out there, we stopped and had a can of beer and some sardines, and then went on, just driving along, enjoying ourselves.

We turned south off the highway there by a grove of trees onto about a two-mile stretch of blacktop road. In the evening light the place looked especially desolate: old beat-up shacks, old log cabins, here and there a farm with an old-style tractor. One tractor I saw was twenty or twenty-five years old. Things were really junky.

We turned west at the end of the blacktop road and went as far in this direction as we could. Then we turned south and drove on, hoping that we could go on into Nebraska, which is not more than a quarter of a mile from where we were. But the road ran out, there at the creek; no more road at all except for one that wound around over the hill to a house. It was a little old shack, really, with about fifteen old cars around it. About ten of them were pulled up very close to the door. At least one of the vehicles, a pickup, was in running condition. I had seen it on the streets in Pine Ridge a while back.

We left then and started back. We saw a very beautiful sunset over two hills, cone-tipped, with Pine Ridge Village in the background. I was sorry that we didn't have our camera. Such a beautiful, desolate land.

We drove on northward to where a white rancher lived. We just stumbled into his backyard, and by golly did that guy have hogs all over the place! The rancher, Ralph Johnson, is a man in his thirties. He was, of course, quite concerned about us coming to talk to him, his place being way out at the end of the road like that. He didn't know who we were or what we wanted. He came out from his yard to inspect us. We visited there with him for a while, talking about AIM and what they were doing.

A lot of people are uneasy these days, especially around strangers. Nobody knows what to expect. Take Johnson Holy Rock, for instance. Now, Johnson is a very stable sort of individual, yet he stood in the council meeting and told of a frightening incident with strangers. Johnson lives away from the road about a quarter of a mile, and you have to wind down through a creek to get there. He was home alone when he saw two real rough-looking characters walking down the road to his house. When he saw them he was frightened. He had firearms in the house, but he said that it had been a long time since he had fought in World War II and he didn't know whether he could really pull the trigger to kill those men if he felt that he must. He was fortunate in that he was able to call the law. Of course the police came and questioned them and ran them off, in accordance with the tribal code, which required that foreign people without specific business are not to be on the reservation.

We left the rancher and drove on down to the Oglala Sioux tribal roadblock. It was dark by the time we got there. There must have been five cars at the roadblock altogether. One was a Roads Department truck with roads poles on it, and some of the poles from the truck had been used to set barricades right across the road. There were also barricades in the ditch on either side, and these were well camouflaged. I don't know why they needed to be camouflaged, but they were, with hay and straw. They had a nice little fire going in back of the log barricades. We came up on them from the side, and the fellow who came out to check us out was cautious and suspicious and was carrying a rifle in the crook of his arm. Someone else came up right away, and this man recognized us. Of course we were then invited down into the pit for a cup of coffee. June elected to stay in the truck.

It was a nice quiet night and pleasant to be visiting with the folks down there. I could hear the crackle of a radio, and they explained that it was an AIM radio that they were listening to. AIM and the Wilson roadblock both have radios supplied by the federal government. There was some good-natured teasing going back and forth in the pit. They were kidding about this being "cowboy coffee." It sure did taste good. You could tell that it was going to get pretty cold before the night was through. I asked them if they were getting their rations, and sure enough, they were. As I said before, we have been bootlegging two cases of C-rations to them every day. I had told the supply man of the BIA police to get it to them.

As we were standing there, a car drove up. The first thing we noticed was that it had but one light. Somebody said, laughing, "This is an AIM car. It has only got one light." It pulled up to within about fifty yards of the blockade, stopped, and began to turn around. One of the guards, with a rifle in the crook of one arm and a cup of coffee in the other hand, walked down the road and waved the car up to the roadblock. It came on up to the roadblock all right, and we could see that it was a fairly late-model Mustang with New York license plates. When the occupants were told to get out of the car and put their hands up, they were really scared. The guard shined the light in their faces: they were fuzzy-haired kids—looked like kind of kooky college types out on a vacation. The guards looked through their trunk and searched them, then turned them around and told them to go back.

Right in the middle of all this, here came another car. It was coming from the left side of the roadblock, not from the front. I told one of the fellows who was standing back along with me (I didn't want to get out there in front too much), "You better watch that one; it could be a trap for you." He did watch it, but it turned out to be one of our own, Glen Three Stars, who was just coming into the roadblock from the other side after a reconnaissance.

The next car that came along was full of Indians. They came right to the roadblock, right up close, and the guard shined the light in their faces. The guards did not search them, just talked to them. They were probably more courteous to them, being Indian, than they had been with the scraggly young white men before. Finally the guards turned them back, too. The occupants of the car said that they had the idea the road to Wounded Knee was open. Of course, we knew that they were lying because their car had a number 65 local county license plate. Being from the area, they certainly knew that the road was closed, so there had to be some other reason for them being out there.

After a while we left and went on home. It was kind of strange to see armed people stopping cars on the Oglala Sioux reservation. It is a sad thing, too, that people must fight each other in this way when there is so much to be done all up and down the reservation. One thing that is very noticeable is that all of the Indians manning the tribal roadblock were mixed-bloods—not a full-blood in the bunch. This further indicates the split between the mixed-bloods and the full-bloods in this affair.

Meanwhile, the "New Nation of Oglala" continues to exist. After we got home from the roadblock, we watched the news on television. Here is their description of the situation:

> Negotiators at Wounded Knee met in a tepee for three hours today to try to resolve the thirty-three-day-old dispute, and told newsmen that talks are at a critical stage. The Indians' attorney said a settlement is very near. The government spokesman said progress has been made, but is less optimistic. The government's chief negotiator said the meeting, the second in two days, discussed in detail a ten-point list of items presented by American Indian Movement leaders of the occupation. The chief negotiator, Assistant Attorney General Kent Frizzell, said a third meeting is scheduled for tomorrow afternoon. As he put it, "Because the nego-

tiations are at a critical stage, I don't want to discuss any individual items."

Chief counsel for the American Indian Movement, attorney Ramon Roubideaux, agreed to Frizzell's assessment of the talks. In response to a question, Roubideaux describes progress in the talks as remarkable. He said that Frizzell had been open in his dealings with AIM leaders, and negotiators are very pleased, and as the AIM lawyer put it, "I think that there is substantial agreement on most points and I think that we can reach an agreement on this framework and that the confrontation is very close to being settled." Roubideaux said when an agreement is reached on the ten-point program, AIM leaders in the takeover, all of whom are under indictment, probably would agree to go to court. Frizzell responded to Roubideaux's comments by saying, "I am not as optimistic as some nor as pessimistic as some." He said that he would have to go back to the Interior Department for authority to deal with some of the Indian demands.

Both of the negotiators say that it is significant that another session is scheduled tomorrow and that the cease-fire would continue. Frizzell said the Indians pressed a demand that the media be allowed into Wounded Knee but the government refused. Frizzell said that his authority for keeping newsmen out is based on common sense, adding that there is armed insurrection at Wounded Knee. Both sides declined to comment on relationships of AIM forces and the volunteer group under the leadership of Oglala Sioux Chairman, Dick Wilson, an archfoe of AIM. Wilson forces have set up their own roadblocks to keep food and newsmen from entering Wounded Knee. Frizzell said between twenty and twenty-five men were seen taking ammunition into Wounded Knee last night. He said they crossed between federal roadblocks number 4 and 5, and two or three men were arrested. Federal officers found one knapsack containing rifle ammunition.

I don't know what these negotiations are. That is the business of the Justice Department. It is interesting that they are talking about ten conditions now. The last time there were only three, the time before that five, and so forth. This is the way it goes. Also, some of these conditions relate to something that the Justice Department has no authority over, so the Department of Interior will somehow have to be brought in as well. We shall see what that amounts to.

April 2, 1973

Monday. A lot of work today. As I mentioned before, today was the day I intended to move the agency operation out to the various communities. That way perhaps we could serve the people a little better than we are able to do in the midst of all this. I talked my plan over with Moot Nelson, the assistant superintendent; Tony Whirlwind Horse, the assistant superintendent for education; and Bob Ecoffey, the tribal planning director. They persuaded me that we should not go out into the community at this time. They said that last night a couple of teachers had been harassed. One of them, an Indian woman, had been stopped and at the point of a gun had been forced to sign a petition before she was allowed to proceed. With things of that nature going on, my three advisers felt that if it became generally known that the BIA was out in an area regularly, this would just invite harassment. So, against my better judgment I called off the move.

I was more successful with another of my projects today. One of the things that I have been trying to get done for quite a while is to get the land records of the Oglala Sioux

Tribe transferred from the Realty Division to Land Operations. Back in the 1950s, management of Indian lands was divided under two offices within the BIA: One office, known as Land Operations, took control of range leases, grazing land, irrigation and range, and soil and moisture conservation. The other, known as Real Property Management, took control of farm and pasture leasing. Over the years the two branches developed in different directions. Land Operations tried to look in terms of total use of the land, overall planning. To this end, over the past ten years they have developed an automatic data processing system (or ADP) which enables them to tell within a tenth of an acre how much land is available for the various uses. The Realty Division concentrated on individual land-ownership records, correct title to land for the individual Indian allottees, and transactions involving individual parcels of land. The problem is that Pine Ridge Realty here is responsible for 1.3 million acres, and with their present system they can't say within 25,000 to 30,000 acres how much total land the tribe and the individual allottees have in the various categories.

Over the years the tribe has borrowed money from the Farmer's Home Administration and other agencies to buy hundreds of thousands of acres of additional land. These loans amount to millions of dollars, and they require that the tribe and the BIA make a better accounting of the land purchased in this manner and of the income it has generated. To provide a way to do this, I have been taking steps to have all the tribal land transferred from the recording system in the Realty Division to the ADP system in Land Operations. So today we actually got going on it. It is a big project and an important one. This is a particularly good time to tackle it, too: the Realty office is full of U.S. marshals; the Credit office is full of FBI; the army is in the Plant Management shop upstairs; the command posts of both the FBI and the federal marshals are in the Roads shop; and the assistant U.S. attorney general and his staff are over in the Employment Assistance shop. Obviously, we are not getting anything done anyway in the line of normal business, so we might just as well be working on this.

A third project came about as a direct result of the crisis here, and that is a count of all the potential voters in the Oglala Sioux Tribe. The tribe and the BIA together should have put together a voter list back in about 1937! Now we need one right away because of a petition that has been circulated by the Oglala Sioux Civil Rights Organization. This petition calls for the abolition of tribal government on the Pine Ridge Reservation, and to be valid, or binding, it has to be signed by one-third of the number of eligible voters in the tribe. So, suddenly the BIA and the tribe are working like mad to go through the rolls and establish a qualified voter list. The folks working on this are over at Hiram Olney's place, the old house of the administering manager. There is no phone over there, and they are really hard at work.

At the briefing this morning, Kent Frizzell sounded very encouraged. He thinks he can get the negotiations pulled together within two or three days and get those people out of Wounded Knee. It has been thirty-three days. He is hoping it can be wrapped up soon because he knows very well that it will soon be spring break at the colleges and some of the college kids may well be looking forward to a Fort Lauderdale of the North. Frizzell talked a lot this morning about the terms of arrest. It seems that in this latest round of negotiations, AIM has presented him with ten proposals. He said that the only one that means anything is the one concerning terms of arrest. Of those occupying Wounded Knee, there are fifty or so who have been indicted, and Frizzell seems determined that those fifty will be arrested and also that no weapons will be taken out of there by anyone. Those who have not been indicted may just walk out and away unless and until they have indictments against them. Of course the residents who have nothing to do with what has happened there will not be bothered in any way.

Frizzell and others in the Justice Department were concerned about how Dick Wilson and his men at the tribal roadblock might react to all this. With some reluctance Frizzell did meet briefly with Wilson and Toby Eagle Bull. A representative of the press was there, too—I forget his name just now—a man from NBC. The question came up again about press coverage of the negotiations. The pressman kept talking about "the public's right to know," until Wilson, Eagle Bull, and I reminded him that up to now the press has not been interested in any facts. It has only been interested in death or the threat of death. No effort has been made to find out what has really been going on, and the tribe has been damaged by this kind of reporting from a preconceived point of view. Frizzell suggested that the tribe and the press might work out some kind of trade: maybe the press could do something for the tribe here in return for being allowed to cover the negotiations. I picked this up right away and asked if NBC would be willing to produce some kind of documentary showing the problems of the Oglala Sioux Tribe and the efforts of the tribal government. Something positive, something that could raise money for tribal development, as other organizations are doing now for AIM. Wilson and Eagle Bull were not impressed. They just said no: "You people have had your chance at truthful reporting. You have not given it; you have damaged us by your untruthful reporting. In no way will we consent to allow the press to go into Wounded Knee for the negotiations."

Frizzell, Wilson, and Eagle Bull finally got down to their discussion. Frizzell did clear with Dick Wilson the principles of arrest procedure. Wilson gave him a commitment that the tribal roadblock would be dropped immediately to allow a reoccupation of Wounded Knee by the government. Frizzell requested that Ramon Roubideaux, AIM's chief lawyer, be allowed to go in for two or three more days, and Wilson agreed to this, but no one and nothing else was to go in: no other lawyers, no food, no baby food, no medicine, no supplies, no ammunition. Nothing was going through the Oglala Sioux tribal roadblock. Actually, Wilson's policy seems to be working pretty well. With no food and no chance to capitalize on press coverage, the AIM people seem to be losing interest. Maybe that is why they are willing to talk seriously about coming out of Wounded Knee now.

In the midst of all the briefings, meetings, and special projects, a strange thing happened today. For thirty minutes I actually worked on something positive for the development of the Oglala Sioux Tribe: trying to get an industry to move in here. This makes the third, maybe fourth, time in the last two months, certainly less than six or seven hours, that I have been able to work positively for the Oglala Sioux people. All of the rest of my work during this period has been defensive in nature, dealing with the problems created by a revolutionary force. These hours have been long. All through February and March I was nearly constantly on duty, all day, every day, and with phones ringing in the middle of the night.

Like this evening, for instance, Wyman Babby called me at home real mad because nobody will tell us what those nine or ten negotiating points are. That is nothing new, because the tribe and the BIA have been completely cut out of all of the significant negotiating for six or seven weeks now. I have mentioned before, I think, that the Justice Department does not listen very much to the local officers of the Department of the Interior and listens none at all to the tribal officials. In this regard, the Justice Department operates like the BIA used to work and still does to a degree. The decision-making process is oriented toward the top: they get their decisions made and squared away with everybody upstairs, including the White House; then they rush out, after the fact, to sell the decision to the people who should have been in on making the decisions with them in the first place. This is exactly the wrong way to go about dealing with anyone! I think I know how it is in this instance, though. These men from Justice talk to AIM constantly and steadily, and they hear about how corrupt Stan Lyman is and how corrupt Dick Wilson is, and they can't help but begin to believe a little bit of it. So, it may be that the Justice Department is becoming convinced that there is in fact corruption here on the part of the local

BIA and the tribe. This was expressed openly by one of the Justice representatives who was in charge here for a while when Harlington Wood went back to Washington. When approached about talking to the tribal representatives, this man said that he could not afford to become friendly with the tribe or to be identified with the tribe, when he might have to prosecute certain members of it. I should have asked him how he could become so friendly with AIM, since he might have to prosecute them also. However, I am not that quick a thinker.

April 3, 1973

Again today, at the morning briefing, everyone was optimistic. Kent Frizzell said it looked like things were finally being wrapped up in the negotiations. He began asking questions about the tribal roadblock. We told him it was a volunteer roadblock. He wanted to know if the volunteers were deputized. We told him no, they were not deputized. Well, what right did they have to be there? No right. Well then, why should he have to put up with them? And, of course, the answer was obvious. I was the one who had to say that we had to put up with them because they are there, just like the Wounded Knee people, who also have no right to be there.

About that time, in walked Dick Wilson. He was concerned about the fact that three people from Wounded Knee had come out with people from the Community Relations Service and they had not been turned over to the tribal police. Frizzell wanted to know why they *should* be turned over to the tribal police. Dick Wilson said that anyone who is in Wounded Knee now or who has been there previously is guilty. Frizzell blew his top at that. I haven't seen a fellow that mad since I can remember. He told Wilson, "I am going into Wounded Knee this afternoon, and when I come out of that place I am not going to be guilty, and if your judge wants to see me in court I will see him in court, but he won't be the judge—he will be a defendant!" Wilson couldn't say much in reply. None of us could, I guess. So Wilson walked out, just left.

I went downstairs alone and began working on something else. I spoke briefly with Dick Wilson, who said, "I don't believe that I deserved this." Everyone agreed that he did not. He then went on his way with the intention of calling the attorney general of the United States to have Frizzell removed. Pretty soon, along came Charlie Soller, from the solicitor's office, saying that they wanted to see me. I broke off quickly from what I was doing and went to see Frizzell and Soller. Frizzell said, "I have made one hell of a mistake. I had no right to blow my top that way. Would you call Dick Wilson and see if he would let me come over? I will apologize to him." So I called Dick and told him what Frizzell wanted, and Dick said, "Well, I guess we all blow our top once in a while in these trying times. Send him over." Dick was about to call the attorney general when Frizzell came over to the tribal building to apologize. Frizzell's apology seemed sincere. It was certainly straightforward. You have to give Frizzell credit for correcting the mistake he made. I mentioned before that I have noticed various people losing their composure all along, and when Frizzell lost his, I thought, "Well, here is another one." Anyway, he may pull it together now.

Another important thing that happened today was that I gave an interview to a fellow named David W. Hacker. He is from Cairo, Illinois, and represents both the *National Observer* and the *Wall Street Journal*. He was asking about the governing body of the Sioux Tribe. Some good points came out in the interview, so I am including part of it here.

> SL: The governing body of the Sioux Tribe, known as the council, is composed of twenty individuals who are elected, according to population, from eight separate districts within the exterior boundaries of the reservation. There is also an executive committee, which operates during the interim

period when the council is not in session, and this is once every quarter.

DH: Does the council have a specified length of meeting?

SL: No.

DH: Like a week?

SL: No. The executive committee is composed of the president, or chairman, and vice president of the Oglala Sioux Tribe, who are elected at large from all of the tribal membership.

DH: So it is a two-member executive committee?

SL: No, it is a five-member executive committee.

DH: Five-member?

SL: Yes. When the council takes office it elects three more members of the executive committee. These can be chosen from the general population or from the council. These members are the secretary, the treasurer, and the fifth member. In the case of the present council, the treasurer of the executive committee is also a member of the council.

DH: But the secretary is not.

SL: Right. The executive committee meets whenever there is need of it. They can be called into a meeting at a very short notice.

DH: What are the responsibilities of the council?

SL: To represent their people under the constitution of the Oglala Sioux Tribe. The other day I was under probe from another reporter and found myself hard-pressed to name the kinds of services this council provides that another city or state government would provide—like streets and police protection—things of this kind. Those services are provided by the BIA. In other words, in a state or county government, police protection would be provided by taxation. Here the council provides that same protection through contract with the BIA, not through raising money through its own taxing process. The BIA then becomes the instrument for providing the services which an ordinary governing body provides for its citizens.

DH: So the BIA provides the streets, the police protection, the sewage, the street lights, and other municipal services.

SL: Most of it. Some of the sewage protection and some of the electric power are provided locally, but mostly it is provided through the BIA.

DH: To whom, then, is the BIA responsible? Or is the BIA responsible to the council?

SL: Yes, the BIA is responsible to the council, and, of course, it is also responsible to the BIA hierarchy. For example, our Law and Order Division would be a case in point. The Bureau of Indian Affairs runs the police department through an agreement with the Oglala Sioux Tribe. I guess it is more than an agreement. It is tradition. It is one of the obligations of the BIA, that they will provide police protection. There was a time when the Oglala Sioux Tribe ran the police department themselves. They gave it back to the BIA. Even though they were running the police department under contract, the obligation still remained with us to provide the service. We provided the money for it. Your question was, are the actions that a tribal council performs subject to approval by the BIA? Was not that your question? The really interesting thing about it is, yes, they are. For example, recently the tribe passed an ordinance in relation to the unwanted foreign individuals on this reservation. One of the first things that the BIA had to do was find out who had the approval authority on this ordinance. I have forgotten who ended up having it. I believe that it was the area director, my boss. Sometimes this authority is with the assistant to the secretary of the interior for Indian affairs. The point is that there was no question that the ordinance would be approved by the BIA. The question was, just *who* would approve it. In the old days the superintendent would have taken a look at it, and he would have decided that maybe he didn't want to approve. There is an established procedure for him to go through if he does not wish to approve. The rules spell all of this out. But nowadays, in this climate of relationship between the tribe and the BIA, there was no question about it being approved. It was just a matter of whether or not it was legal, and if it was legal, okay, it would be approved. So the question was how soon and who does the approving—not should it be approved. I think here is the really significant turnaround in the relationship between the Bureau of Indian Affairs and Indian tribes throughout the country. This turnaround has taken place in the last ten or fifteen years. There are many, many Indians and whites who do not recognize that this has, in fact, taken place. This is a question of the way the government deals with the Indian tribes, as against the way the government deals with Indians as individuals.

A good example of the way the BIA has related to the tribe, as against the individual members of the tribe, can be found in the land-sale policy. It used to be that the Bureau of Indian Affairs encouraged the sale of land owned by Indian individuals. This was in the fifties. Since the fifties the policy has been for the tribe to purchase the land, if possible. Basically, the policy has been to prevent Indian land from going out of trust. Flowing from that, you have to decide who is going to buy the Indian land. Well, it can only be another Indian or it can be the tribe. If the tribe buys the land, you see what happens. You have a shift from a group of landowners who are members of a tribe, to a group of landless Indians who are members of the tribe which owns the land that these landless Indians have sold. So down through the years, at other places and here, the BIA has been encouraging the purchase of the individual Indians' land by the tribes. This creates a captive market, because the tribe is the only one that can buy. It means that an Indian cannot sell his land to the highest bidder if that is a white man, because the BIA is not going to let it go out of trust. The BIA will insist on it remaining in the hands of Indians. The BIA does appraise, but it seems quite clear that the land is going at less than it would bring if it were to go on the open market. So here is a case where the BIA is clearly oriented to the best interest of the tribe, as against the best interest of the individual member of the tribe. As I face this myself, in my own conscience, it is quite easy. If we sell a ten-thousand-dollar piece of land from an Indian to a tribe, that individual takes the ten thousand dollars and uses it for good or not. The purpose of his use is beside the point. In any event, the money is gone very soon, and the Indian is landless. Eventually, he dies, and the situation is forgotten. The land which goes to the tribe goes to a legal entity that goes on forever. It is just like the church or the state, which is ongoing. So what if you could have gotten two thousand dollars more for that individual? You place that against the fact that you are preserving forever the land in ownership by Indians—right or wrong.

The day ended on a very bright note. Frizzell and Roubideaux made a joint statement to the press in which they said they were in agreement on all but one point. They felt that

Wounded Knee 1973
A Photographic Record

Stanley David Lyman as an administrator with the Bureau of Indian Affairs. *(Stanley D. Lyman Photograph Collection, Special Collections Department, University of Utah Libraries)*

Senators George McGovern (center) and James Abourezk (right foreground) speak with an unidentified
woman who has learned of the firebombing of homes
in Wounded Knee on March 1, 1973. (UPI/*Bettmann
Newsphotos)*

Overleaf:

At negotiations in a tepee (left to right): Leonard
Crow Dog (foreground), Dennis Banks (with chin on
hands), Russell Means, unidentified, Ramon Roubideaux, Kent Frizzell. *(Stanley D. Lyman Photograph
Collection, Special Collections Department, University
of Utah Libraries)*

AIM supporters celebrate in front of the Gildersleeve
store in Wounded Knee. (*UPI*)

(Above): Stanley Lyman (center, wearing glasses) observes the Wounded Knee area from one of the several bunkers that surrounded the village. *(Martin Lyman photograph)*

(Right): Almost three weeks into the occupation, armed militants escort a car carrying Harlington Wood, assistant U.S. attorney general, to a checkpoint as he leaves Wounded Knee after meeting with AIM leaders. *(UPI/ Bettmann Newsphotos)*

Oglala Sioux Tribal President Dick Wilson (center) stands with armed civilian volunteers at a roadblock set up to prevent aid from reaching the militants in Wounded Knee. The Wilson, or tribal, roadblock was about three miles outside the main federal roadblock. (UPI/*Bettmann Newsphotos*)

Two of the fifteen occupiers arrested at the end of the takeover. *(Stanley D. Lyman Photograph Collection, Special Collections Department, University of Utah Libraries)*

U.S. marshals examine Molotov cocktails found in Sacred Heart Catholic Church after the AIM supporters left Wounded Knee. (*UPI*)

AIM leaders Russell Means (left, seated) and Dennis Banks (in leather vest) at a victory rally in St. Paul, Minnesota, after charges against them were dismissed in September 1974 after a trial lasting eight months. *(UPI)*

BIA Area Director Wyman Babby (left) and Stanley Lyman at the Abourezk hearings on the events of Wounded Knee. *(Martin Lyman photograph)*

they could surely come to an agreement soon. But then again, how many times have we heard that before?

April 4, 1973

I think that today can be characterized something like this: as far as the negotiations at Wounded Knee are concerned, they are "exactly the same as they were yesterday, except better." Anyway, that is the word we got back from Kent Frizzell, who was out doing the negotiating with AIM today.

One good sign is that last night, for the first time, they caught people trying to sneak *out* of Wounded Knee. Usually it is the reverse—they are trying to sneak in. Three FBI agents heard them down in a draw, sneaked in there after them, called for a flare, and there they were, nine of them. The agents yelled at them to put down their guns, and they all did. These nine people were Indian residents from other reservations, the FBI said, except for one, who was an Oglala. They were carrying quite a lot of weapons, and they were carrying the "scrub list." This is a list of people who, we are told, need to be done away with. Wyman Babby, Dick Wilson, and many of the so-called "goon squad," (that is, Dick Wilson's volunteers), are on the list. I am on it too. There is speculation as to what those nine men were doing out of Wounded Knee. They suggest three possibilities: one is that they were coming out to make an attack on somebody; another is that they were coming out to attack the Wilson roadblock specifically; and the third is that they may have seen that the end was near and were just trying to get out and get away.

Also, we found some dynamite today—a dynamite bomb up by Shangreau's store. I don't know all of the details on it yet, but they say that it was well made, that the person who made it knew exactly how to do it. They are still looking into the circumstances surrounding it.

Much of the time today was spent figuring out how we are going to get into Wounded Knee when the negotiations close. It is going to be something like this: The FBI will go in and make a sweep for booby traps, land mines, and things of that kind. They will separate the Oglala residents of Wounded Knee from the nonresidents. The residents will just be identified as residents and turned loose. The nonresidents will be fingerprinted, and except for those who have warrants against them, they will be turned loose too. There will be an assessment of each house for damages. We are going to have three people in there with cameras to do nothing but take pictures. Everyone is excited about going into Wounded Knee after these thirty-five long days. We shall see.

Another thing on my mind today was the petition against Dick Wilson and tribal government. There were 1,450 or so names on this petition, and it was presented to me about two weeks ago, very carefully, by a committee and Mario Gonzalez, who is a local legal-aid lawyer and a member of the Oglala Sioux Tribe. June and I knew Mario's mother during World War II, when she was a young woman. She went to Rapid City Air Force Base and got married. Since then she has lived away from the reservation all of her life, so Mario is basically a product of urban living.

As I said before, a petition of this kind must be signed by a third of the eligible voters of the tribe. There had been approximately 3,000 votes cast in the last election, so everyone assumed that the 1,450 signatures they had were well over the required number. What they did not figure on, evidently, is that if the secretary of the interior were to call for an election on whether or not to abolish tribal government, as the petition demands, he would be required to include eighteen-year-olds in the base. Previously, those under twenty-one years of age had not been included. Just yesterday we were finishing the count, from tribal rolls, of all Oglalas, and we found that there are 9,300 Oglalas of age eighteen years and older. Thus, the number on the petition would have to be around 3,100 or so.

Unfortunately, I didn't have this final figure yet when Mario Gonzalez came to see me yesterday, accompanied by Louis Bad Wound, one of the local people who had helped to

circulate the petition. The three of us reviewed the instructions given by the secretary of the interior for, first, determining whether an election would be held and, second, for
holding it. As we read those instructions Mario quickly saw
that it could well be that when the count was completed,
the 1,450 signatures on the petition would not be enough.
He was concerned, because he stated flat out that the reason
why things were quiet around here lately was because people
felt that they were going to be able to get rid of Dick Wilson through this petition and the subsequent election, which
would destroy the constitution of the Oglala Sioux Tribe.

We talked a bit about what would take the place of tribal
government. We agreed that there would have to be an in-
terim administrator of some kind. For example, on 400,000
acres of land it would be ridiculous to get over half of the
members of the tribe together to sign each lease. This duty
would very likely go back to the BIA.

I asked them about what kind of government would take
the place of the current tribal constitution. They were very
nebulous about that. It would be headmen and the old chiefs,
they said. "How would they be selected?" I asked. "Well, they
would have to be elected." Of course, there would be no ma-
chinery for electing these people because it would all have
been abolished along with the constitution.

As we talked along, it became quite obvious that these two
men—a smart young lawyer and a conservative, middle-aged,
not too informed Oglala Sioux—were consumed by hatred
for one particular individual: President Dick Wilson. All they
were interested in was getting rid of Dick Wilson. To them
he was an autocrat, a dictator; he was crooked; and they were
willing to sacrifice a constitution to get rid of him!

Today, now that our count has been completed, I have to
figure out how to announce that the number of eligible voters
in the tribe is *six times* more than the number of names on
the petition. Of course I am the one who has to make the rec-
ommendations to the secretary of the interior as to whether
or not the petition is any good. Toby Eagle Bull and Dick Wil-

son were really laughing about that. One good thing about this whole situation is that it forced a count of the tribal membership. Now, at least, if the Oglala Sioux Tribe does in fact wish to put their enrollment together, they can do it. We have done the work; we have brought it up to the point where they can take official action to place these people on the rolls and to establish an ongoing permanent roll.

Interestingly enough, from this number of over 9,000 people eighteen years of age and older, it looks like there could be around 20,000 Oglalas in all. It was great to see the reaction when I gave this figure to two Oglalas. One was Toby Eagle Bull, the secretary of the executive committee. Toby said, "Oh boy! That is great! I am not going to worry about these other challenges now. This is great! I am going home, and I am going to get the first good night's sleep I've had in weeks." The other was my boss, Wyman Babby, the BIA area director. Wyman said, "Oh! That is wonderful! Do you realize that is 20,000 people, 20,000 of us?" I said, "Sure." Then he said, "I just can't believe it. That is wonderful. Pretty soon we will be as big as the Navajos." So here you see at work the intense Oglala pride, which unfortunately, now, in these times, has been channeled into hatred and into carrying guns and into destroying constitutions.

April 5, 1973

Well, today was the day! The siege is over, after thirty-seven days of occupation. I stood on a hilltop overlooking Wounded Knee to watch things wind down. Others were there with me: my son, Marty; our secretary, Jo; Bob Carlow, former fifth member of the Oglala Sioux Tribe executive committee. Mac, the communication man from the BIA area office was there, busily taking pictures. Ski Jacobs, BIA police captain, and Lou White, BIA special officer from the neighboring Rosebud Reservation, were there, watching from a police car. Federal marshals and FBI agents were there too. We could look down and see Wounded Knee in the distance and the cars coming out of there. As we watched, a helicopter landed, blue and white and skinny, making a lot of racket and kicking up a lot of dust. Russell Means got out of one of the cars and was arrested by George Tennyson, U.S. marshal for South Dakota. Handcuffed, Means got into the helicopter, a U.S. marshal on either side of him. Ramon Roubideaux, his attorney, climbed in with him, and the helicopter took off. It was good to see Russell Means in handcuffs, finally, after all this time, submitting to arrest. After days and days and days of heartache and hunger and anger and dissipation of forces that could have been used in a positive fashion, I couldn't keep back the hatred and the glee when I saw that man finally submitting.

Out at the tribal roadblock everybody was busily dismantling the place, packing things up. They agreed to tear down their roadblock as soon as an agreement was signed, and they were holding to it. The men at the roadblock were friendly, really in a holiday kind of mood. Some of them asked me to take their picture; some of them wanted me to shoot their gun; some of them didn't want to let me through. The days of waiting were over for them, too. Working men, mixed-bloods, each one with a stake in the mixed-blood society of Pine Ridge: the status quo, the system that would never change. They like it like it is; they came here ready to kill and be killed because they wanted to keep it like it is.

There was quite a hassle out there. The poles that were used for the roadblock belong to the tribe and were hauled out there by a BIA truck. So today we had to get another BIA truck to go get them and haul them back. This roadblock had taken fire at least twice from AIM people who had come out of the Wounded Knee perimeter. But the shooting had been from a long distance, and evidently, none of it had hit the roadblock directly, because there were no bullet holes in those poles.

Standing at the tribal roadblock were three Red Cross trucks, white and red with blue lettering, shining brightly in the sun. For days the Red Cross has been trying to push themselves into the forefront, to be the first ones in there to serve the people. They were there giving out sandwiches: a red cross on the paper sandwich bag, a red cross on the paper cup that held the coffee and the orange juice. They were first all right—first in relief, as they had wanted to be all along and had maneuvered so much to be able to do. They have done their duty; they will be able to get more donations because of this. Yet the relief that the Red Cross will contribute, in terms of dollars and cents, will be much, much, much less than the quiet relief that will be given by the BIA Social Services under the leadership of Jere L. Brennan, a skinny, unassuming young man, a mixed-blood, with a master's degree in social work.

The sun was low in the Pine Ridge sky when I came back to the town. I would have liked to go home and get a drink, but I wanted to hear what would be said to the press about the peace agreement, so I decided to stick around for it. I suddenly realized that something had left my shoulders, and for a moment I wondered what it was. But then I knew; I soon recognized it: there was a time when I was sure that in the next half hour, or half day, or in a day or two, someone would be killed—maybe myself—from the involvement I had in this affair, from an order that I gave. Now that load was gone because I had survived; the whole reservation had survived without anyone being killed! In my joy and relief at this feeling, I said this aloud in the office.

Then I saw the cloud in Jo's face as she said quietly, "Leo was killed." The BIA policeman who was there with us spoke up too: a quiet man from Yakima, Washington, there serving his guard, doing his job. He said with great seriousness, "There are two new graves at Wounded Knee." I don't know whether or not he is right. If he is, then whose are these graves? I thought about the other acts of violence, the ones we know of. I wondered what happened to Goings, the young man who was shot through the leg. What happened to Enos Poor Bear's son, who was shot through the hand—not a very bad wound? What happened to the Chicano medical volunteer who was nicked with a bullet? Where are these people? Why have they not come out? With marshals with high-powered scope rifles, firing tracer bullets directly into portholes, there must have been some killing. I am well aware that the BIA policeman could be right, and what he said has left doubt in my mind. Whether right or wrong, I know that the rumor will persist forever, the rumor that "there are those who died at Wounded Knee." Certainly, the feeling that Leo was killed by AIM will be carried in the minds of those who remember as long into the future from this Wounded Knee as it is back to the first Wounded Knee. With these dark thoughts, the thoughts of the killing which did take place or probably did take place, the weight settled back on a little bit, and I was not quite as glad as I was before.

The signatures of the AIM members on the peace agreement included many familiar names and some not so familiar.

Russell Means: Charisma, brilliance, hate, purposefulness —all of these traits this young man has, and what a waste that this skill could not have been harnessed together with that of the BIA and the tribe instead of being pitted against them. An urban Indian, a lost man, perhaps, in that his heritage is only a remembrance, a faint one, of what it really used to be. But to him now it is sincere, this heritage. No longer is it faint. It is proud and bright and takes its form in defiance toward established forms of government.

Tom Bad Cob: We had never heard of him until today. I am told that he is an Oglala.

Clyde Bellecourt: A Chippewa, one of the principal leaders of AIM. We know little about him except that he is either loved or hated.

Hoksila Wakan: It seems that Clyde Bellecourt is using this name in reference to himself, but this has to be a put-on. *Hoksila* means "young," and *Wakan* means "spirit." Why should he sign himself as "Young God" in Sioux?

Pedro Bissonette: He looks like a man of Spanish ancestry, but his last name, "Little Bison," speaks of French ancestry as well. A mixed-up, lost young man, who wanted to do so many things at Pine Ridge for the young folks: boxing matches, youth camp, youth groups. And then he got into trouble—knocked down a state welfare worker and threatened to kill him with a rifle. He fled from arrest and, as I mentioned before, in doing so hit Special Officer Hi Price with his car. Price will never be the same again for his injuries. Pedro was out on bond from this charge when he decided to join the Oglala Sioux Civil Rights Organization. And there he is at Wounded Knee, one of the signatories of the peace agreement.

Carter Camp: A Pawnee from Oklahoma, I believe. Big, tall, a good-looking man, violently angered. I did not know him before except from his pictures. Another man of charisma.

Wallace H. Black Elk and Grace F. Black Elk: I'm not sure who these two are—descendants of the great Ben Black Elk, perhaps.

Florene Hollow Horn Round: An Oglala whom I don't know personally, but I know members of the family. I knew Stanley Hollow Horn during the war when he was trying to make a living as a ranch hand up in Newell, South Dakota, an alien in his own land. His brother, Oscar Hollow Horn, had been a friend, had helped me make the decision to come here to Pine Ridge. Now he is alienated from us—accused us and the marshals of shooting at women and children in Wounded Knee.

Karen White Butterfly: I don't know anything about this woman.

Crow Dog: He has a first name, Leonard, but he seldom uses it. A Rosebud Sioux; he has no business here at Pine Ridge.

Gladys Bissonette: Perhaps a relative of Pedro.

Delilah Bean: From Fort Peck, Montana; probably a relative.

There was other business today as well, mainly telephone calls. I talked to the chairman, Dick Wilson, this afternoon. I told him I felt he should go to Washington to the hearings on

Wounded Knee. He just laughed and said, "People are telling me that I listen to you too much." The chairman doesn't like to ride in airplanes, and he doesn't really feel comfortable outside of the mixed-blood society of Pine Ridge. So I knew he was reluctant to go to Washington even though he knew he ought to. Johnson Holy Rock called with a complaint. His Laundromat had been vandalized twice. The first time it happened, he called the police and he never could get them. The next time, the police did come over but only after quite a while. They gave the excuse that there were only two of them on duty. What could I tell him? Most of the marshals and the visiting BIA police have been at the roadblocks. Our local BIA police force has been hard-pressed to do whatever ordinary business needs to be taken care of. We did get the authority to put on fifteen extra men, which brings the police force here up to thirty, but what we need is fifty. Helen Schirbeck called for Secretary Weinberger of Health, Education, and Welfare. What could her department do? she asked. I could not think of much except to suggest that perhaps HEW could send a team of specialists here to spend six months or so developing programs that would fit the needs of Pine Ridge, deal with the social forces which have been unleashed here, and make another Wounded Knee conceptually impossible.

This evening we learned that five hours after his arrest Russell Means was free again, on a twenty-five-thousand-dollar bond. The money was put up by a man from Rapid City, someone I had never heard of before, but it sounded like a white man's name. Tonight Kent Frizzell held a press conference to talk about the peace agreement. "There are no winners," he said, and how right he was. There truly are no winners. The government has a hollow victory in the fact that Russell Means was arrested. AIM has a victory of sorts, too. They get publicity out of it and a visit with a representative of the White House. This meeting will take place Saturday, day after tomorrow, and Russell Means is already making capital out of it. Now he is saying that unless things go to suit him in that meeting, he will not give the order to have arms

laid down at Wounded Knee, which is contrary to his agreement with Frizzell. So it may not indeed be over. In fact, it
will never be over for a long, long time to come. These forces
which have caused people to shoot at each other in anger have
not changed in direction or feeling just because a cease-fire
has been signed. I hope tomorrow won't bring any trouble or
any more shooting. There was some shooting today, at the
very time the agreement was being signed. We think it was
accidental, men just shooting off their guns or maybe just target practice. I am skeptical, but it really could be over. We
all hope that it is. Maybe now we can get some work done. I
don't know. I sure hope so.

April 6, 1973

Today is the day when disillusionment has set in. It happened
after a visit from Gilbert Eagle Thunder (pseudonym). Gilbert
Eagle Thunder: full-blood, the man who said about twelve
years ago in a bar in Los Angeles, "Don't call me Gil; my
name is Gilberto." Now he wears a headband and is a member
of the tribal council. He talks for and about his people and
was one of those who carried the fight against Dick Wilson
in the council. I had been friends with him after he came to
see me with the rest of the Oglala Sioux who came to Utah.
Gradually I had lost his friendship, as I had Oscar Hollow
Horn's and others'.

I sat and visited with him today, and he talked about what
is needed in tribal government. As he talked I realized that
this man has known for a long time what I have come to know
only in the last few months: that tribal government is an
overlay; it does not reach the people. He described the situation better, more clearly than I had seen it for myself. And as
he spoke, suddenly he was crying. He was embarrassed for a
time; he paced the floor, and I gave him a Kleenex. Then he
went on, with words and thoughts that are too personal to be
detailed here: his ideas about Indian government and Indian

life. It had to do with wanting to be a full-time councilman, a councilman with an office, one who could mingle daily with his people, talk with them, find out what they need and help them. It had to do with the concept of the boss farmer, which went out of style thirty years ago and yet is still very much with us today. It had to do with the desire of the Indian to be a stockman on his land and how there is no way for him to do that, just as there is no way for most of us, whites as well, to be stockmen on the land that we owned in western South Dakota. Economics has caught up with us all, white and Indian alike. The crying didn't stop and I wished it would. I understood some of what Gil Eagle Thunder was telling me, but there was nothing I could say, no way I could express to him that I did understand, nothing I could do to help. Finally, he said, "I guess you can see I hurt for my people." And his face, an ordinarily beautiful face, now contorted with pain, was like other faces of grief and pain I have seen all too recently in this community.

Disillusionment. Yesterday we watched Russell Means fly away flanked by two federal marshals. Then he was bonded out and was on his way to Washington, making statements to the effect that he would not give the order to lay down arms in Wounded Knee until the White House conference turned out the way he wanted it to. The White House conference, as it happened, was not to be in the White House. It was in the National Center for Dispute Settlement, as if the dispute had not in fact been settled! Frizzell evidently began to realize that he had been taken, and all of the plans to go into Wounded Knee in triumph, with the Indians laying down their arms, are zero tonight. Means had agreed in negotiations here that he would give the order to lay down arms *when the meeting in Washington began*. Now it is clear that the order may not be given at all and that the Indians are not going to lay down their arms tomorrow or anytime soon.

When the word came through about all this, Mr. Moore of the FBI was sitting there in the command post, and I had to say to him, laughingly, "Well, I have to laugh at you. You really got took again!" And he said, "You should laugh *with* us! We've all been taken. These are revolutionary people; they follow the advice of known revolutionary factions, and they are proceeding now in a way—a typical revolutionary way—which has been known to many of us for many years." And of course June says she had told me that very thing a year ago at the time of the first AIM intrusion. I myself said it too a year ago, and I really got kicked in the pants from our central office for saying that these folks act like trained revolutionaries.

The Red Cross went into Wounded Knee yesterday. The AIM people there said, "Where were you when we needed you? What are you doing here now?" They were searched and were told to wait. While they were waiting some young men began siphoning the gas out of their vehicles. The Red Cross representatives said, "Please! Leave us enough to get back out of here!" And they did. Then more AIM people came and took all of the food contained in the three trucks, fifty-five cases of it, and stored it in their commissary. The Red Cross man I talked to said that they were well organized. I asked if they were going to lay down their arms. He said that his impression was that they certainly were not. The Red Cross said also that there are 250 people presently in Wounded Knee and 150 of them are armed.

I had lots of visitors today besides Gil Eagle Thunder. I had a meeting with Del Eastman and Dwight Mirable, who are in charge of the local BIA police. Once again the question of the assassination list was brought up. They think that such a list does exist and that perhaps Del and I are on it, along with Wyman Babby and Dick Wilson. They are not sure—there is no proof of it—but they think so. We also talked over a serious problem concerning the police force. While the negotiations were still going on, AIM kept complaining about four officers of the BIA police force. Because of this complaint, Frizzell and Marshal Colburn have ordered these four officers to be temporarily transferred to another location, in hopes of defusing the present explosive situation in Pine Ridge. We in the BIA decided that these particular officers are there when we need them. They are on duty; they respond, maybe a bit aggressively at times, but they are good officers, and we cannot sell them short. We all agreed that the only way these men would be removed was for someone in the BIA line of authority to tell us that they must be removed. We will send that word back to Marshal Colburn, and we think that will be the end of it.

Right in the middle of this discussion, we got word of an altercation three or four hours earlier involving one of those very officers: Glen Three Stars. It seems that Glen had been harassing Hobart Keith and Hobart shot him in the face with mace and then pulled out his gun from under his coat. He shot a hole through the coat and into the ground. We don't know whether he was really trying to kill Glen Three Stars or whether the firing was accidental. At any rate, Hobart Keith was arrested on a federal charge—assault with a dangerous weapon—and tonight he is in jail. Hobart Keith: brilliant, talented, an artist, some say deranged, hating to be in jail but in jail nonetheless.

I had a visit from a newspaper reporter, a nice young man from way out in Los Angeles. I gave him an interview. After that, along came Ed Stover and Paul Apple, who are tribal councilmen. Paul Apple had been beaten up by some AIM people about the time Leo Wilcox was killed. He said, "I am afraid to go back home to Manderson. I think I will come over and live in your root cellar over here." And Stover said, "I'm his gunner." "What do you mean, his gunner?" I asked. "I mean, I sit in the backseat with a gun, and if anybody is coming from behind I will shoot him, like we did in the war, from a tail-gunner position." I don't know how much he was joking and how much he was serious.

We visited for quite a while. What they think should be done is to sue the United States government for not having done its duty in protecting life and property at Wounded Knee. It is not a bad idea, really. We finally decided that there are two ways to go about it: One is to sue the United States government for every conceivable loss to the Oglala Sioux people which has resulted from not properly handling the Wounded Knee situation. The other is to go through Congress with a bill to pay for the damages to the individual Indians, to the non-Indian owners, such as the cattlemen, and to the Oglala Sioux Tribe. Also, enough money would be put into the package to enable the Oglala Sioux Tribe to purchase the forty-two acres at Wounded Knee on a negotiated-sale basis. We all laughed, but we agreed that we would let Dick Wilson and Toby Eagle Bull know about this and that we would be guided by the Oglala Sioux tribal attorneys, Dick Shafter and Bobo Dean, on which of these routes we would take. Later, in talking with Wilson and Eagle Bull, I found that they,too, were in complete agreement. So it could well be that we will really move in this direction. It is something which has been in the back of my mind for quite a while.

Today, April 6, was the end of the fifteen-day period during which challenges could be made against the petition filed with us to abolish tribal government here at Pine Ridge. Well, at 4:28 this afternoon Toby Eagle Bull, Verle Akers, and Bogie Amiotte walked into the office with just such a challenge. And quite a challenge it was, too! They were quite friendly themselves, but the letter they brought challenged everything we did. It really took after us—the BIA, the superintendent, the Pine Ridge office. I don't know if they meant it or not.

In the midst of all these meetings and visits today, I had an unusual phone conversation. Michael Spotted Bear called collect from Yankton, South Dakota. I don't ordinarily take collect calls, but I also want to be pretty sensitive to what they might be. When the fellow said he was from Yankton, I knew that he had to be from the state hospital and I thought I'd better find out what he wanted. He said, "I am a patient at Yankton Hospital. I earn $151 a month in social security. The tribal court committed me here. I have my social security money in the Individual Indian Money Bank, and they are taking $100 a month out of my social security money to pay for my confinement here in the hospital. Since I am confined against my will, they should be paying for it and not me. What can you do about it?" I didn't really know, and I told him so. He said, "Thank you," and hung up. Jo, who was listening in, said, "Now that is the most sensible person I have talked to in three weeks!"

April 9, 1973

Monday morning. Lots of notes on my desk and bits of news. Rumor has it that AIM claims most of their coming and going in and out of Wounded Knee is done at the site of the BIA bunker, implying, of course, that we are the weak link, the ones not doing our job. Another rumor is that a photo newsman who somehow got into Wounded Knee was kept prisoner there for a time, chained to a chair. He was finally released and was either sent out or allowed to go out. Needless to say, he was very disheartened by his experience. He was evidently questioned by the FBI, but we in the BIA know nothing more. Another note: The Wounded Knee perimeter is nine miles square, and within that area two hundred individuals own land. What a lot of damage and inconvenience this confrontation has brought to those two hundred people and to many others besides. People like Orville Cuny. I received a letter from him this morning dated April 2. In it he describes how he was run off the road last March 10, out south of Scenic. He had had an argument with some AIM people, and when he drove off they followed him and purposely ran into him from behind. His car went off into the ditch, and the AIM people in the other car just drove off and left him. Someone else came along and helped him and took him back to town, but he had to leave his car. He came back a couple of hours later to get the car out of the ditch and found that all the windows had been smashed, deliberately beaten in. Orville felt certain that AIM had done it.

This morning we had a meeting of just the BIA staff and

tribal officials. We had important business to deal with: school-enrollment figures, training for school board members, other questions concerning education. We also had a progress report on the transfer of the land records of the tribe to the automatic data processing system in Land Operations. Both Moot Nelson and Gene Egglesten assured me that it would be completed in a matter of days. Once these records are complete, we can move ahead with a $2.1 million loan which we hope to get from the FHA. With that money we can buy back sixty-six thousand acres of Oglala Sioux allotted land which has been sold through the years to whites. Another serious financial matter was the question of payment on a note at the Stockmen's National Bank in Rushville, Nebraska. Something has to be done about it before May 1. This was a $90 thousand loan taken out by the Oglala Sioux Tribe under the administration of Gerald One Feather, the tribal chairman who preceded Dick Wilson. The principal on this note is still $70 thousand. When we asked Dick Wilson why this had not been taken care of, he reminded us that his administration inherited not only this debt of $90 thousand but also another debt of $159 thousand owed to the Internal Revenue Service. Except for $28 or $29 thousand in penalty charges, this sum represents money which the tribe withheld from paychecks but which Mr. Clark, the tribal business manager under the One Feather administration, did not pay to the IRS. Despite all the controversy over Dick Wilson's administration and his management of financial matters, maybe one administration is about the same as another, after all.

After our own staff meeting I went over to the briefing meeting with the Department of Justice. Poor Kent Frizzell! He has really been snookered! Of course, old pros like Toby Eagle Bull have been saying all along that this is the way it would turn out: AIM will negotiate forever; they will change negotiators; they will change points on which to negotiate; anything to drag things out. The representatives of the Justice Department, true to form in ignoring the legitimate tribal officials, have paid no attention to this point of view. So here we are now, a big deal in the newspaper: Wounded Knee is over, negotiations successful, when in fact the government representatives have been taken in by the promises of AIM. In a way, Frizzell really did an excellent job in being able to actually get an agreement from AIM, to tie them down to some real specifics. Knowing their methods in this kind of situation, I think this is a real accomplishment. As a result of Frizzell's efforts, AIM was forced this time to actually break an agreement instead of just shifting around, like they usually do. Unfortunately, the public will probably never know all this because somehow the news is always on the side of those who are trying to overthrow government. Consequently, AIM's side of the story will be told very effectively in the news; the government's side will be told very ineffectively. In any event, Kent Frizzell will be back in the field today, talking to the occupying force in Wounded Knee, talking to new negotiators on new points of negotiation. He mentioned a new five-point proposal.

I am rather unpopular around here because of my opinion that the Justice Department should be dealing in this crisis with the duly chosen officials of the Oglala Sioux Tribe rather than with the insurgents. Today, for example, I tried to arrange a meeting between Dick Wilson and Stanley Pottinger, assistant U.S. attorney general, Civil Rights Division, who is here to replace Frizzell. I got very little interest. I don't know what these fellows in the Justice Department relate to, but it certainly isn't Indian business. We have never seen the like of it before. Justice Department representatives can come and go, and all the while, the judges of the Oglala Sioux Tribe and the president of the Oglala Sioux Tribe are still being ignored.

In the meantime, the negotiations go on, and I just wish we had the money that is being spent here to use for the Oglala Sioux Tribe instead. This would be enough money to run a good law-and-order program for three, four, maybe five, years, instead of a very poor one; enough money to put five hundred jobs in Pine Ridge; enough money to put hundreds of houses in Pine Ridge, the kind we want and need. But we won't get that money because it will have all been spent just trying to maintain the status quo. As soon as this thing is over, as soon as the problem is settled in accordance with the wishes of those in Washington, we will not be listened to again, the same as we were not listened to this past year, after the first AIM intrusion.

I had a very interesting discussion today with Johnson Holy Rock. He was twice president of the Oglala Sioux Tribe, but not in successive terms. (No president of the tribe has ever succeeded himself.) Johnson came to see me because he was unhappy with the way he had been treated by the people in the Judicial, Prevention, and Enforcement Service (JP&E), formerly known in the BIA as Law and Order. Dick Colhoff, who is a good friend of Johnson's, is being replaced as special officer in this department by Del Eastman. Johnson had tried to get to see Del Eastman, but Eastman had paid no attention to him. Johnson is a very respected man in the tribe, and he is not used to being treated in this offhand kind of manner. He was really angry. He came over to see me to find out what it takes to get an appointment with new Special Officer Eastman. He had wanted Del to sign a permit so that he could buy a gun with which he could really protect himself. While we were waiting for Del Eastman to see him, we had a chance to visit a bit. Here is a man, a full-blood, born in 1918, who has put together a viable economic operation and made himself a real power in the community. He is very, very perturbed about what is going on in this country; he is afraid for tribal government; he is afraid for what is going to happen to the thinking, sensible people of the Oglala Sioux reservation. He told me of two incidents involving official meetings within the apparatus of tribal government, and I think they are significant.

Back in November of 1972 there was a meeting in the town of Oglala of the survivors of the first Wounded Knee, the one eighty years ago. The purpose of this meeting, which Johnson Holy Rock attended, was to see if there was some way to recompense them for all their trouble as survivors of the Wounded Knee of 1890. Those attending the meeting were thinking, intelligent, interested Oglala Sioux. The meeting was disrupted by two young men. They came into the meeting hall and told the people there, "You have no power; you have no voice. No one will listen to you. You meet, and that is all. Join AIM and we will be strong; we will be powerful. We will force the government to listen to us, to deal with us." They harangued the old folks and insulted them. They went from one to another, and finally they came to Johnson. The young man said, "Who are you?" "I'm Johnson Holy Rock." "Well, that's great. Who's Johnson Holy Rock?" So Johnson told him and asked in return, "And who are you?" Johnson didn't remember the name which the young man gave him. One thing led to another, and finally the young man taunted Johnson: "What are you going to do about it?" Johnson said, "Well, maybe I'll ask you to leave." And the young man replied, "Well, just try it. You can't put me out of here." So Johnson hung up his coat and started for him, but the young man backed away, and kept backing away until he backed into a group of women who urged him out with the advice, "Don't cause any trouble." He stood in the doorway and cursed Johnson, and then finally he left and his companion followed him.

The other meeting Johnson Holy Rock told me about was held at Porcupine. Johnson was not there himself, so he reported it to me secondhand, as he had heard it from Charles Under Baggage. Charles Under Baggage is also a former president of the Oglala Sioux Tribe and is the current president of Oglala Sioux Tribe Landowners' Association. The way Johnson described it, the meeting began in much the same spirit as the one at Oglala. They were talking about grazing regulations. This is a very important issue to the Oglalas who own land and also to the whites and mixed-bloods who lease that land. Significant numbers of acres are often involved, and even though the grazing revenues are not enough to make the landowners a living, that income, whether it is five dollars, or five hundred dollars, or twenty-five hundred dollars, is still a significant amount of money to them. So they are interested in grazing regulations and in the amount of money that they can get from leasing their land.

These matters were being seriously discussed when suddenly the place was inundated by large numbers of young people who hooted and made catcalls and ridiculed the old people, saying again that they would not be listened to, that the meeting was meaningless. Now, Charles Under Baggage is a very dignified man; he is not too knowledgeable, perhaps, in the economics of the day, but he is steeped in knowledge of the old treaty rights, and he wears the cloak of sincerity about him. Charles Under Baggage was probably beaten down completely by the rude young intruders because his English is not as fluent as his Lakota; in fact, he doesn't speak English very well. These younger individuals who were taking over the meeting would have had little knowledge of Lakota, but they would have had enough power in their English and enough persistence to utterly subdue the quiet Indianness of Charles Under Baggage. Charles did assert himself, finally, and he said, "This is our problem, these grazing regulations. This is what we are talking about. Do you people have the knowledge to deal with this problem, to understand it, to help us with it?" And he gave them the documents containing the grazing regulations. They looked through them and made no comment. They threw the papers on the table and left. But the meeting was done for, completely destroyed.

In relating what occurred at these two meetings, Johnson Holy Rock's point—and he made it clearly—was that the thinking, sensible people of Pine Ridge will not be meeting anymore; they will not be holding meetings and talks again. And it is a great pity and a great disservice for everyone concerned.

I found a bit of encouragement later in the day in the visit of the three people who had spearheaded the petition to dissolve tribal government: Louis Bad Wound, whom I have mentioned before; Delores Swift Bird; and Barbara Means. All three of them have been determined that tribal government has to change, but in talking with them now, I find that they have a new perspective. They originally started the petition to abolish government specifically for the purpose of getting rid of Dick Wilson. Now, after the heat of the original action, they are saying that what they really need is a change, a true change in tribal government. For the first time, these people seem to realize that the problem is not a particular person— not a particular tribal president, a BIA superintendent, or a BIA area director. Their problem is what the Oglala Sioux people do with the government they have.

April 15, 1973

I spent April 11 through April 14 at the special BIA conference in Brigham City, Utah. It was a pleasure to get out of here for a couple of days and to work on problems that I am somewhat removed from instead of problems that are staring me in the face every day. The purpose of the conference was to discuss plans for dealing with other AIM intrusions and plans for training a BIA support force, similar in conception to that of the United States Marshal Service.

On the way home, I was waiting at the Salt Lake City airport for my flight back to Rapid City when I had an interesting encounter. I ran into Gerald One Feather and Helen Schirbeck in the airport lobby. Gerald, as I have said, was president of the Oglala Sioux Tribe before Dick Wilson; and Helen, a good friend and business associate of his, has quite a powerful position with the Department of Health, Education, and Welfare. For a while she had considerable power with the BIA, too, and under the Bruce administration was a candidate for one of the very top positions in the Bureau. As I have mentioned, I have talked to her on the phone, but I had never met her in person before this.

Gerald was telling me about the Meade hearings last week in Washington. He said that he himself had been kept on the stand for five hours. His opinion was that the Justice Department and the federal establishment had made a mistake and had created a confrontation situation at Wounded Knee. I was not going to let that pass, so I asked Gerald what he would have done in the same situation, a situation where AIM had occupied a location, had drawn the battle lines, had fired at people coming in—in other words, a situation where AIM had in fact created the confrontation. It was the first time I had ever seen Gerald One Feather without an answer. Usually his mind is so keen and his thinking is so quick that he has an answer for every question you could ask him. This time, however, he had no answer.

As the three of us were visiting there, I looked out through the open door and saw one of the AIM-type people coming across the airport parking lot to the lobby where we were standing. Just seeing him made the resentment well up inside me. This is a strange, strange thing that has happened in the business of Indian affairs, as far as I am concerned. Time was when I would never have had that kind of reaction toward an Indian—any Indian—and here I felt resentment toward this individual because he was dressed in the way AIM members dress, which almost amounts to a uniform. As I watched, the fellow came in and stopped to talk to a couple of black fellows. Then I noticed a man whom I recognized as an FBI agent standing around close by, just looking around. Then this AIM individual talked to several other Indians waiting in the airport, some of whom knew me and had talked to me before he came in. At one point he and his group came close to where Gerald and Helen and I were standing, and I sensed a similar kind of tenseness in them, too. There was a real gut-level reaction on the part of both Gerald One Feather and Helen Schirbeck. I could just feel it, and of course I recognized it as the same sort of feeling I myself had had previously when I saw this man walking toward me. It wasn't fear; it wasn't hate; it certainly wasn't love. It was just an intense awareness; we were all extremely conscious of this man and of his group. I guess what this shows is that many of the AIM people are very powerful, charismatic individuals who do attract attention and who make their presence felt wherever they go.

As this group moved away, the conversation I was having with Gerald and Helen broke up, and I went over and talked to the FBI agent, a man I had known for quite a while. I would not have approached him except that he had said hello to me. As soon as I spoke to him, I could see that he did not want to talk to me. I got the impression that he was there to watch this group. He did tell me who they were, though. The very charismatic Indian fellow was Clyde Bellecourt. He had recently come out of Wounded Knee, just in the last two or three days. He had submitted to arrest and had in fact been arrested but, of course, had soon been bonded out. His stated purpose was that he had come out to Utah to raise money for AIM. One of the men with Clyde Bellecourt, the FBI agent said, was the militant black activist Stokely Carmichael.

As I drove back home tonight after flying into Rapid City, I noticed at least fifteen or twenty FBI cars going from Pine Ridge to Hot Springs. These were men coming off duty, some of the same men I had seen driving into Pine Ridge as I was on my way to the airport the other morning. I was surprised then at the amount of traffic, and I wondered for a moment if something special was happening. Then I realized that this was just the normal coming and going of men reporting for work, manning their posts in this situation of crisis. That morning and again this evening, I couldn't help but think of the amount of traffic and money which has flowed through this small community of Pine Ridge since the AIM intrusion.

One of the things that has happened since I've been away is the establishment of a new roadblock outside Wounded Knee. Now, as before, only one of the official roadblocks, roadblock 1, is designed as a checkpoint through which people are allowed to enter and leave the perimeter. Dick Wilson's tribal roadblock had been set up to block off roadblock 1 so that it was really the Wilson roadblock which controlled who and what went into Wounded Knee. As I have said, the Wilson roadblock was dismantled as soon as AIM agreed to end the occupation. Now, the former residents of Wounded Knee, the ones who have been displaced by the AIM intrusion, have become unhappy with the way the Justice Department and the federal government have been handling the situation. So they have set up their own roadblock to replace the Wilson roadblock, in the very same spot.

I haven't talked to these people yet, but I will probably go out there and see them tomorrow. They are talking about charging the federal government one hundred dollars a day for the inconvenience they have faced during what is now forty-five days that AIM has been sitting in Wounded Knee. Moot Nelson was out talking to them today, and they asked if we could supply them with some of the portable toilets we have for handling crowds. I told Moot that we could send them out some and that we could also supply them with C-rations. This probably isn't exactly what we should be doing, but we will probably do it anyway. It is certainly no worse than the Justice Department's having allowed all kinds of equipment and food and supplies to go into the AIM fortress. From what Moot tells me, the representatives of the Justice Department are just tearing their hair over this new citizens' roadblock. They can't stand to have this illegal roadblock sitting in front of *their* roadblock, but there is nothing they can do about it. The roadblock by Wounded Knee residents may be illegal, but the Justice Department has tolerated an equally illegal road-block by AIM for some forty-five or so days now. Whichever way they go, whichever action they take, the Justice Department is caught because they have been unable to eliminate the AIM roadblock.

April 16, 1973

Today was a real interesting day. It was one of those days, I guess, when you could say with all honesty that even if you had a million dollars and did not have to work, you would have liked to be doing exactly this today. Having been away most of last week because of the Law and Order Conference in Utah, I was pretty much out of touch with what had been going on at home. I called a staff meeting. I had come back from Utah with nearly a quarter of a million dollars worth of surplus federal equipment waiting to be distributed, so we talked in the meeting about where it should all go. We also talked about the citizens' roadblock. Dick Hellstern, deputy assistant U.S. attorney general and second in authority of the Justice Department representatives here, is apparently going to try to get a court order to have it removed. Mike Windham, our BIA area special officer, told him he'd better not do it. These are just ordinary people, people who are mad because the Justice Department has not done its duty out there. I also learned that the land inventory for the $2.1 million FHA loan is finally completed. The inventory that had been promised last week and about every week now for a year is truly finished. A good job done, finally. Also, in the meeting, the branch chiefs have been directed to make an inventory of the losses sustained in their individual branches as a result of the present AIM intrusion. This has to be in by Thursday.

After the staff meeting I went upstairs to talk to Bill Hall, who is second in command here of the U.S. Marshal Service. I learned that there has been a change: All of the marshals are now working at the roadblocks, except roadblock 1, which is manned by the FBI. The BIA police have been replaced by marshals at the X-ray and Zebra bunkers and are now on patrol. Our special officers, Mike Windham and

Del Eastman, told me that that was okay as far as our law-enforcement people are concerned.

About this time, I called and left word with Stan Pottinger's secretary for him to call me when he had a moment, because I needed a briefing from him on what had happened in my absence. A few more phone calls and then another meeting with the executive board of the Oglala Sioux Tribe. Dick Wilson, Toby Eagle Bull, Bob Ecoffey, and others were there. We addressed the question of a recreation project for the tribe in connection with the Badlands and made a little progress. We also discussed the housing projects at Denby Dam, Calico, and Manderson. Some big problems there, with no way to handle them in a meaningful manner.

I left the meeting and went back to my office. Still no word from Stan Pottinger. I called Hill Air Force Base in Utah to tie down the surplus equipment we had been promised and then turned my attention to a demonstration of Oglalas going on outside the building. Word had come in that fifty cars were on their way to the reservation to support the group demonstrating here and that Ramon Roubideaux was in one of them. Fearing real trouble here, the police had assigned us extra officers, who were standing in the hall outside my office. They said that they intended to serve warrants on all nonresidents, including newsmen and civil rights attorneys, just to get them off the reservation. I decided I had better go out and talk to the local group before any of this came to pass. I told one of the policemen where I was going, and he said, "We'll watch you." I told him, "Well, okay, watch if you must, but I don't really feel the need of it."

When I went outside I saw people that I know—people who are opposed to me but who will still talk to me. I also saw the signs, saying things like "Wilson, We Don't Want You!" and "Down with Tribal Government!" I tried to find out what their grievances were, what was behind this particular demonstration. They told me frankly, "You don't know what's going on here." And I said, "Well, I am here to learn." They explained, "Wilson's goon squads are after us; they have been harassing us." "Sign a complaint against them," I said. "But it doesn't do any good to sign a complaint," they objected. I said, "You've always said that. Why don't you try signing a complaint and let us see what we can get done." "No, it's no good," they said, "the complaint would not be honored." Once again it was evident that these forces in opposition to the system haven't even given the system a chance. They are evidently unwilling to face up to the real problem, to take positive action, and to follow the procedures within the system that would get things done. Yet there is no question about their sincerity.

After a time, I went inside with Louis Bad Wound, Barbara Means, and Delores Swift Bird, three of the main petitioners in the attempt to abolish tribal government. I called in Jim Clear, our departmental solicitor, to confer with them. In their discussion it became clear that the three petitioners were well informed and had thought things out pretty clearly, for the most part. They must be getting some good legal advice somewhere, since they were able to make their points, some of them technical ones, quite clearly to this bright young lawyer from Washington. The points at issue had to do with the time of filing, the number of eligible voters, the enrollment of tribal members as of 1935, and the challenge to the petition by Toby Eagle Bull.

Three others—Hildegard Catches, Pete Catches (the medicine man), and Eddie White Wolf—came into the meeting too, and in the enlarged discussion some really fine things came out. This discussion was particularly gratifying to me since these three people dislike me intensely, Hildegard Catches especially. She has gone on radio and television and written letters in the attempt to get me out of the Pine Ridge Reservation. At one time she insulted me in front of a council meeting. Still, she sat in my office and talked with me positively about problems and how to solve them.

In the midst of this discussion, I finally got word from Stan Pottinger, or rather, from his secretary, asking me to please get the air-conditioning fixed. My word to the secretary was,

"I will not respond to such a request until Mr. Pottinger responds to my request, which is now about four hours old, for just a few minutes' briefing from him on what has gone on in my absence." So then Stan Pottinger, the great man from the Justice Department, came down the hall to my office and said, "We've got to get together." "Yes," I said, "we've got to get together, but right now Hildegard Catches and her group here want to see you. Where could we meet?" He mentioned the conference room, but it was full of pressmen at the time. So I suggested that we meet in my office, and I asked if he objected to my staying with him. "Oh, no," he said. "No, that's fine. Just stay." Once we all got into my office we were short one chair. I stepped out to get another chair, and Stan Pottinger shut the door behind me and left me out. Well, I'm kind of pushy, you know, so I opened the door and brought the chair in and gave it to someone, and then sat down myself and started to listen. Of course, Pottinger was very uncomfortable about this, but I could see that the Indians felt good about my being there—even my enemies—so I was more than willing to stay.

Hildegard Catches and Louis Bad Wound told Pottinger that they represented six out of the eight districts on the Pine Ridge Reservation and five or six organizations, among them the Interdistrict Council, the Landowners' Association, and the Oglala Sioux Civil Rights Organization. They presented Pottinger with a list of grievances, but mostly what they wanted was for Pottinger to act as a go-between between them and Russell Means. They were now out of communication with Means and wanted Pottinger to tell Means to please talk to them before he and his people went on with any further negotiating. They made it clear that AIM was in Wounded Knee at their invitation and that now the situation had gotten out of their control. This whole thing was difficult for Pottinger to understand. With all due credit to the lawyer minds of the Justice Department, they just cannot grasp the intricacies of local tribal politics. Neither can we, of course, but they seem to be much more inept at it than we are. All things considered, Pottinger did very well. He said, "Well, I cannot force Mr. Means to talk to you, nor would I try to force him, but I will tell him what you want. I accept your presentation of these documents, which are your list of complaints, and I accept your idea that the law-and-order problem at Wounded Knee is related to and has resulted from the inadequacies of local tribal government and from other community forces at work in the Pine Ridge area."

Then Pottinger left since he had a briefing meeting to attend. I wasn't invited, of course, but I knew where and when the meeting was being held, so I could have gone. They would not have dared to turn the Bureau away from it. But I wanted to talk some more with the delegation of Indians there in my office, so I stayed behind. One of the things that had happened while I was gone was that Charlie Soller, one of our departmental solicitors, had asked those heading up the drive against tribal government to put together something positive, to state what *they* wanted in terms of tribal government. There at that meeting, we went on to discuss their efforts in that direction. They told me how they had worked all night, way into the morning, and had become utterly frustrated, had just thrown their papers in the air and said, "We can't do it." Then they started over and had finally put together a document incorporating their vision for tribal government at Pine Ridge. What they said went something like this: "Every organizational chart that we see for tribal government has a commissioner or a president at the top and the people at the bottom: a pyramid, from many to one. This is wrong. We want to start differently; we want an inverted pyramid, a wedge, with the people at the top." And on the document they gave me, there was the Sioux word for "the people" at the very top. They went on to explain that the Pine Ridge Reservation would be divided into seven districts. The people of each of the seven districts would select a representative from their district. The term *select* here instead of *elect* is significant. There was to be none of the white man's elected way in this process: the seven district representatives would be selected in the Indian way, ways which involved the pipe and which, they said, would ensure the selection of individuals truly sensitive to the needs of their people. Even the *eyeskas,* or mixed-bloods, they said, would see the wisdom of the Indian way of representation and would go along with it.

These seven district representatives would then form a body called the people's council, which would run the affairs of the tribe much in the way that the present twenty-man council does now. Under this council they listed all kinds of programs: building maintenance, health, roads, law and order, public relations, education, and others. Actually, their concept of a form of tribal government which would reach down more to the people was not too far from the one which I had envisioned myself, except that as a non-Indian I could not understand their method of selecting their representatives. We talked about this, but I did not convince them that an election would be the fairest way to select the people's council, nor did they convince me that a truly representative form of government could be achieved by the application of the Indian way among what would surely be a minority of people in each of the various districts. We talked this over back and forth and then I said, "Look, do you really want to go back a hundred years? Do you want to go back to the times when either I or someone else in this position will do all your business for you? Because if you abolish tribal government, that is what will happen." They laughed and said, "Well, we will let you stay for another six months, and you can do that. By the time that six months is up, though, we will have our problems of tribal government all worked out and then you can go." I was glad to hear them say that, and proud and glad that I had stayed to listen to these people instead of going upstairs to the briefing meeting. We parted on quite friendly terms.

As I walked up the hall, heading home, I saw a whole group of new people in the conference room. I looked in, and I didn't recognize anybody except our area special officer, Mike Windham. I stepped in, and he introduced me to forty-six border patrolmen who had come into the area to support the

U.S. Marshal Service in their effort to contain the situation at Wounded Knee. I couldn't keep from saying, "Well, since we've got a 'new nation' here at Wounded Knee, I guess we've got a new border to guard. Welcome!" Somehow, it wasn't too funny.

Walking on home, I thought of something else I found out today. I had learned at the morning staff meeting that one of the tribe members, Lawrence ("Prunes") Ecoffey, had died while I was away. I remembered Prunes from a long time back: middle-class, opinionated, sure of the ways things should work, or at least the way they worked in 1940. He had problems with AIM within his family: some liked AIM, some did not. About ten months ago I gave Prunes his high school diploma. He had dropped out years before and then had been in and out of the special programs year after year through the forties and fifties. Finally he stuck to some of the programs in the sixties and early seventies and earned his high school diploma twenty-five or thirty years late. I was proud to shake his hand when he took that diploma because he and I both remembered times, situations, and people going way back to the time when he should have gotten it from someone else's hand. And now he's dead, and there will be another funeral at Pine Ridge this week.

April 17, 1973

This morning the firing started early, about 1:30 or so in the morning. Of course it was all begun by the occupants of Wounded Knee. A few hours later, around 5:00 A.M., two light airplanes flew in and dropped supplies by parachute, in a total of seven different drops. The drops were observed quite closely through binoculars from the bunkers surrounding Wounded Knee. The material dropped consisted of long cases, cylindrical in shape. The marshals were able to identify the make of the planes making the drops—a Cessna and a Cherokee, I believe—but they couldn't catch them. The FBI helicopter, Snooper 1, did dive down into the area, but it got fired at and pulled out.

Shortly after the drops, about 5:30 in the morning, the firing began in earnest. AIM insurgents were very active outside of Wounded Knee proper, approaching several of the government bunkers and firing on them. It appeared as though they were trying to take over one of the bunkers, but perhaps this strong, aggressive action on their part was designed to cover up some other activity. With all this heavy firing it was inevitable that someone would get shot, and indeed, there were casualties. We are certain that four or five AIM individuals were wounded in this morning's action. Some of them were seen to fall, and the marshals could see them being carried from the field on litters. One man, who was hit a couple of hundred yards from a government bunker, was critically wounded. The AIM people sent out a flag of truce and said that they wanted this man evacuated. They asked for a helicopter to come into Wounded Knee and pick him up. The marshals would not consent to a helicopter landing within the Wounded Knee perimeter, so it was arranged that the man would be brought outside the perimeter by car. He was then picked up by a helicopter and taken to Pine Ridge Hospital. His wound was to the head, and he had suffered massive brain damage. He was flown immediately to Rapid City. We have as yet no identification of the man. He is apparently an Indian and had one dollar and a map of Nebraska in his pocket—nothing else, no means of identification.

It is the casualties in this whole mess that are the most regrettable. Look at the situation: AIM is up against a disciplined force, firing coolly and purposefully and only on command. The men in the government bunkers are well-trained riflemen with high-powered weapons. Under these conditions, although there is sure to be a marshal or two hurt, it is obvious that the folks taking the aggressive action within the perimeter are the ones who are going to be really hurt. That is what happened this morning.

Aside from the heavy activity in the perimeter, things went

along about as usual today. The demonstration against the Lyman administration and the Wilson administration and tribal government in general was still going on out on the lawn in front of the building. I went out again to talk to them, like I did yesterday, but my reception this time was not too good. There were about twenty-five people there today, some of the same folks as yesterday along with a few different ones. I saw Edgar Running Bear, for instance. He was one of the Oglalas who came out to see me in Utah just before I came here as superintendent. I know his father, too, from twenty years ago. His father is now at Wounded Knee. Pictures have been taken of him manning a roadblock against the marshals.

One of their signs said, "Stanley Lyman Has to Go from This Reservation!" and some of them were saying, "Why Don't You Tell Your Puppet Dick Wilson to Resign?" This is such a ridiculous idea that it is hard to confront it seriously. It has to do with a concept that Indians have had for years and years and years, the idea that the BIA runs everything and that in so doing they have all-seeing, all-inclusive power in the person of the superintendent. The fact of the matter is that in recent years the BIA has become essentially the instrument of tribal government. So I said to the group of demonstrators, "Look, you are the ones who elected Dick Wilson. You are the ones who voted for him. He is yours, not mine, and I will never tell him or any other elected officer of the Oglala Sioux Tribe what he should or should not do." They retorted, "But he was bought out: he bought his council out, and he bought his votes." Then I said, "Well, okay, I can't really feel sorry for you if you are willing to sell your vote. The problem is yours, not mine or the BIA's, and the burden is on your own shoulders." Well, it didn't go very well this time, and I left pretty quickly. It was clear that this particular group of people were not interested in listening to what I had to say.

We had four helicopter landings ourselves today. Once, the helicopter even set down on the agency lawn and sent the demonstrators scattering like quail. One of the landings was to pick up ammunition and take it to the perimeter; the others were all to transport individuals who had to go quickly from the command post to the perimeter and back. We had a lot of business today related to the BIA Central Office in Washington. First, a young man from the Tribal Operations division of that office was here to gather information and report directly to the secretary of the interior. His name is Bob Farring. We quickly got him incorporated into the decision-making processes of the Interior Department here so that he can do the job he came to do. We were also requested to send certain information to the Tribal Operations office. The Senate Subcommittee for Indian Affairs had asked for a list of all people in the BIA who are involved with the crisis at Wounded Knee. I listed everybody, from the area director to the superintendent to the branch chiefs to all of the individual staff members involved in any way. Then they wanted to know which organizations were involved here. I put together a list of the organizations, including how many people are in them and who is the head of each. Finally, they wanted to know who were the former great leaders of the Oglala Sioux Tribe. I went over to the tribal chairman's office and looked at the pictures of the former chairmen hanging there, and I just named them off. I sent off all this information, as requested: raw, basic information; lists of names with no background supplied, no interpretation. How can this kind of information be put to a valid use? Yet, it will go from a superintendent to a Tribal Operations officer in Washington, and from there to a Senate subcommittee; and this is the kind of information on which decisions will be made. It appalls me to think of it.

I talked to my boss, Wyman Babby, and I sensed a coldness toward me that I haven't seen before. I don't know exactly what it is, but it is something that has developed in the last two or three days. It may have something to do with what seems to be a movement among the tribal chairmen of the Aberdeen area to have Wyman removed as area director. So Wyman has his problems, too, and maybe he thinks that I am part of them. I hope not. I hope that he can see that these are problems that officials like area directors and superintendents always have in times like these.

Tonight I went to a dinner meeting for the Action Task Force of the Title VIII, or dropout-prevention program for the reservation schools. The purpose of these meetings is to gather together people who are meaningful in the local power structure so that they can decide what is going to happen in the community. The concept is a pretty good one, but tonight only half a dozen people were there. Still, there were some good points raised in discussion, and some progress was made toward financing a newspaper through the high school that would really be responsive to local needs.

One of the interesting things about this evening was being in the company of an ex-superintendent who, I believe, was a BIA line officer longer than anyone else in the history of the Bureau. Now that he has retired, I think I have been a line officer longer than anyone who is currently in the BIA. I go back to 1955, but to him, I guess, I'm just a youngster! I got the idea that he was just sitting there laughing at me in all this mess we're in. And rightly so, I suppose. Anyway, it was great fun to have him with me tonight.

April 18, 1973

Quite a lot of reaction this morning to the vigorous AIM offensive of yesterday. For one thing, a new weapon was brought in for use in the bunkers, a KM-79 grenade launcher. It will be used to fire chemical-agent grenades at anyone who comes up close enough to threaten the bunkers, like they did yesterday. For another thing, in the regular 9:00 A.M. briefing meeting, the people from the Justice Department suggested for the first time, absolutely for the first time, that Wounded Knee should be evacuated by force. For the past forty-seven or so days they have steadfastly held to their policy of negotiation, even while Toby Eagle Bull, Dick Wilson, and others have maintained that negotiations would never be successful. Now there is talk of going in and using force to get them out of there. We got word that three houses were destroyed today in Wounded Knee, belonging to Paul Kills in Water, Charlie Moose, and Paul Red Star, all anti-AIM people. The identity of the man who was evacuated yesterday by helicopter has still not been released, although I'm sure the FBI knows who he is. He is about forty-five years old, they say, and is probably one of those who came in just a few nights ago. He was still alive when he reached the hospital in Rapid City, but it doesn't look very good.

Dick Hellstern, second in command here for the Justice Department, is still concerned about the citizens' roadblock, the one manned by displaced residents of Wounded Knee. He sees this "illegal roadblock" as evidence that BIA law and order has completely broken down in the Pine Ridge Reservation and that accordingly, the secretary of the interior should declare a state of emergency and dissolve tribal government here. When I reminded him that I was the one in charge of the police force here, although it is run by Del Eastman, he took a new tack. Since the residents of Wounded Knee were in violation of the law by continuing their roadblock, the BIA police had better go out there and arrest them and break up the roadblock. He wanted us to take care of it, not the FBI or the marshals, despite the fact that the Justice Department had made themselves the supreme authority here and as such are really the ones responsible for any law-and-order breakdown.

Hellstern was also unhappy with Dick Wilson and the tribal government. Wilson would not talk to him, he said; he was getting absolutely no cooperation from the local police force; just nothing was going right. I was trying to make him see that the communications breakdown here was also a result of the Justice Department's way of handling the situation. They have been the ones all along who would not consult Dick Wilson or let him in on any of the decisions that were being made. They did not consult with the local BIA officials either, except when they were forced into it. So they had brought this on themselves. Right at this point in the discussion, Moot Nelson came in and said that representatives of the citizens' roadblock wanted to talk with Mr. Pottinger and Mr. Hellstern and would like an appointment with them for four o'clock that afternoon. I said, "Well, gentlemen, this is a great opportunity. Here is your chance to renew acquaintances with the tribe and begin a little bit of talking." So they agreed to the meeting.

Unfortunately, the meeting was a disaster. Pottinger and Dick Wilson went over to meet with the delegation of Wounded Knee residents and hear their complaints. Pete Swift Bird was there, and Paul Red Star, Toby Eagle Bull, and several others, whom I did not know. They told us in no uncertain terms that we had better get in there and clean that AIM bunch out of their homes and their town. Toby Eagle Bull accused the Justice Department of trying to maintain a bright public image as a successful negotiating force when in fact they were ending up looking like monkeys. Paul Red Star, who is a retired lay preacher and community leader, wanted to go in and pray them out. He wanted to take five people with him, go into Wounded Knee, have coffee with the AIM folks and smoke the pipe, and tell them how they felt about having their homes occupied. He was sure that they would come out. The others there did not think that this would work. They reminded us that their roadblock was to be set up for twenty-one days; seven of those days were gone already, so if in another fourteen days their town was still occupied by intruders, they themselves would go in with guns and move them out.

This was too much for the Justice Department. Of course they couldn't tell these people what they had told us at the briefing meeting this morning, that they, too, were now considering the use of force. Peter Swift Bird indicated that there was going to be trouble here over the weekend. He told of rumors that people who had gotten out of Wounded Knee were gathering their forces in Rapid City and would be back here in a few days. Incidentally, this corresponded to the stories that we were hearing about thousands of people coming to Wounded Knee for a kind of second Woodstock. Our secretary, Jo, was warned by one of her friends from AIM to take the rest of the week off if she possibly could. Well, the meeting didn't really get anywhere. Pottinger got to yelling at the Indians, and the Indians got to yelling at him, and everything just broke up. It was a general no-good session all around. Most unsatisfactory.

June had told me at noon that some of the women who have been demonstrating every day outside the agency were planning on leading a group into Wounded Knee. As I said before, she has her own sources of information. I did not pay much attention to this at the time, but sure enough, they went. About thirty-five or so women, of various ages, went out to roadblock 5, which is on the way from Manderson to Wounded Knee, and proceeded to walk on by the marshals and into the perimeter. Of course the marshals yelled at them to stop, but they didn't; they knew they were in no danger of getting shot or even shot at. The women went on walking in, carrying signs of "Dick Wilson, We Don't Want You!" "We've Got to Have Stan Lyman off This Reservation!" "The U.S. Marshals Are Killing Indians!" "My Heart Is at Wounded Knee!" and things like that. The marshals rushed after them and handcuffed and arrested as many as they could. They arrested twenty-two of them, I believe, but the rest just ran away. These twelve or fifteen women managed to get on into Wounded Knee and are there now. One of the public-information officers, a fellow named Cadeaux, went up to the marshals' office to Wayne Colburn and his second in command, Bill Hall, and really told them off over the way the marshals at roadblock 5 had handled the situation with the Oglala women this afternoon. I don't know what he thought they could or should have done—arrest all of them, maybe, I don't know. Anyway, he told them what a stupid job they were doing. The marshals, understandably, got pretty mad themselves and reminded him that he was one of those fellows who comes out here and is around for about a week and thinks that makes him an expert on tactics. Cadeaux came downstairs and said he guessed he wouldn't be around much longer. He is probably right. I would bet that tomorrow will be his last day on this assignment.

I had a chance to visit with Del Eastman today, our special officer in charge of all the BIA police here. Del is doing a fine job in these difficult times. He himself is a GS-8, and he has men with grades of GS-14 working under him, and I think he handles things beautifully. I was asking him what it is really like out there on the perimeter. He told me that none of the marshals want to be seen with him because he is too visible a target. You see, he always wears a red cap. Well, Del is kind of a gung ho fellow, and he doesn't care much if he is a visible target or not. Besides, he has always said that none of the AIM folks would be a good enough shot to hit him, red cap or not. Yesterday when all of the firing was going on, Del was sitting in front of one of the government bunkers looking down into Wounded Knee with field glasses. The AIM bunkers were about eight hundred yards away. All of a sudden a bullet hit the ground about eighteen inches in front of his feet, throwing dust and sand all over him. He got up and got out of there; he took up a new position by the armored personnel carrier. He was standing there, again looking toward the AIM bunkers with field glasses, when another bullet hit about three feet from his head and ricocheted off the APC. So Del decided that there was somebody down there who could shoot pretty straight after all.

After I left the office tonight, I went over to Hiram Olney's old place, where the girls are still working on the list of qualified voters. Today was the day I was supposed to have it done, and it's not going to be done. I'm pretty unhappy about it, but everyone is working overtime and doing their best on it. To help out, Moot Nelson took home a stack of stuff to work on, and I brought home the names under P to count. There were 525 people in the list that I counted, and of that number, 240 are residents of the Pine Ridge Reservation. It will be interesting to see how the total number of residents on the reservation stacks up against the number of signatures on the petition to dissolve tribal government.

It's a beautiful night. A hard rain has washed the place. Everything smells clean. The first thunder of the year, and black clouds off to the north.

April 20, 1973

We had a little flap in the office this morning with respect to news coverage and reporters. A few weeks ago a correspondent for ABC named Ann Kastner had made a very uncomplimentary report about Pine Ridge on national television. It was one of those things where she was shown standing in front of a row of nice government houses and was reporting that the rich Indians of Pine Ridge lived here, while the rest of the community was dirty, stinking, and poor. I did not see this report myself, but evidently it ruffled a lot of feathers, and there was a lot of antagonism toward her in the Indian community, especially among the women. When Jo told me that Ann Kastner was here today, I sensed a great deal of hostility there, both in her and in Nina Vassar, who also works in our office. I went into the pressroom to talk to Ann Kastner but she wasn't there. A crew from ABC *was* there, so I asked the person in charge—a nice-looking, bearded young man named Dan Harmon—to come into my office for a conference. He very courteously agreed, and I told him of the objections locally to the report of this particular ABC correspondent. Jo detailed the contents of the report for him, since he said he hadn't seen it himself. About that time Arta Carlow asked to say a few words as well. She is presently a member of the school board and is a former member of the Oglala Sioux Tribal Council. She, too, was here in protest of Ann Kastner. Dan Harmon was a bit taken aback by all of this and asked what he could do about it. We made the point that this correspondent had reported erroneously in several respects and that it sounded to us like she was reporting erroneously on purpose. If ABC were indeed interested in reporting the truth, we would give them the facts to correct that earlier broadcast. For instance, one of the things that Ann Kastner had said was that all of the businesses in Pine Ridge were owned by non-Indians, and of course this is far from the truth. Dan Harmon asked if we could give him a list of the Indian-owned businesses in Pine Ridge, and I assured him that we would.

By then Harmon had to go to hear the press conference being held by Stan Pottinger from the Justice Department. He left to get the ABC camera crew set up, and I was called back to the office. The next thing I knew, along came Ted Meredith from the solicitor's office in Billings, Montana, one of the lawyers here to advise the BIA. He said that Pottinger was concerned because the Indian women were giving Ann Kastner and ABC a bad time and were holding up the press conference. I went in myself and saw Ann Kastner sitting over by Stan Pottinger's desk. She was a nice-looking woman between thirty and forty years of age—seemed very efficient, very professional. She was the butt of constant jibes and remarks from the gallery, coming from people like Bessie Cornelius, Jo's mother; Lenore Wilcox, Leo Wilcox's widow; and Arta Carlow. The Indian women were saying things like "What do you folks see when you come out here for two weeks?" "Where do you spend your time?" "Why do you report things like you do?" This went on for quite a while, and finally Bessie quieted them down and the press conference began. I watched Ann Kastner then, and she appeared to be a pretty decent sort of reporter. The questions she asked were very similar to those I have seen being asked by the national television networks. As she was questioning Pottinger, she looked back at some of the women who had been heckling her, and the look that she flashed them was full of as much hate and contempt as any I ever saw. But she quickly concealed it and went on with her interview.

Later in the afternoon I began to wonder out loud where

ABC was and why they had not come to get the list of Indian-owned businesses. All I got from Jo and Nina was the "buck-skin curtain," so I knew that something had happened. The "buckskin curtain" is what we jokingly call it when Indians just quit talking. It can be because you quiz them too much, or because they don't trust you, or just because you are not an Indian. Anyway, that is what I encountered in the office when I asked about ABC. Finally Jo and Nina did let me in on what happened, although they wouldn't tell me who was in on it. It seems that as the ABC contingent was leaving the building, there just happened to be a number of women standing around very close to Ann Kastner, in the hallway and on the porch. And suddenly all of those women had business to do on the other side of where Ann Kastner was, and in going, they "accidentally" jostled her and pushed her and bumped into her, and let her know the scorn with which they regarded her. Needless to say, that was the end of the day as far as ABC was concerned. They did not come back to retrieve the information which we had promised them.

We had another meeting involving the press today: a meeting between press representatives and some of the displaced persons from Wounded Knee. It was rather difficult to get the press interested in hearing what these individuals had to say, largely because the press did not yet realize that there were displaced persons. Finally we did get them together, but not without a forty-five-minute delay during which each group was waiting for the other in a different room of the building, and tempers were flaring. Almost another disaster. The victims of the destruction at Wounded Knee eloquently de-scribed what they had lost: livestock butchered or stolen, family pets killed or left to die, personal possessions used and ruined, houses burned. When one of the newsmen seemed to imply that the citizens' roadblock was acting irrationally, the leader of the displaced residents manning that roadblock re-minded the press corps that it was not the roadblock that had caused all of the shouting, but rather AIM and the response of the Department of Justice. After a time, I felt that the press was no longer listening to these people. They stopped taking notes, and it seemed like nothing more was going to be accomplished.

Right after that session, the leader of the citizens' roadblock, who had spoken so expressively, came to see me in my office. His problem was that on the roadblock, he was carrying a gun, and he was worried about being arrested for it. He had been convicted for a felony and had served a term in prison; he had been out of prison for about three years and was now not allowed to carry firearms of any kind. I suggested that he could be in command of the roadblock without personally carrying a gun as long as the others there were armed. He reminded me that shots had been fired at the roadblock and at him and that he could not go out in the dark to inspect a car without being armed himself. He thought that somehow I, as the superintendent, could go above the law in this case and somehow get him permission to carry a gun. When I could not, he just informed me that he *would* be armed when he was on the roadblock but not at any other time. Here is a man who has been trying to work his way up to a decent life and who has now lost everything. He is a counselor for the alcoholism program and has been saving up for a trailer house. He finally saved enough for the down payment and got a nice eight-thousand-dollar trailer and had it set up at Wounded Knee about three months before the AIM occupation. Now, of course, his trailer and all of his personal belongings have been destroyed.

Right now there are about nine families, with about 60 persons in all, still living in Wounded Knee proper. There are about seventeen families that live on the perimeter of the occupied area, and they keep going in and out. There are about forty-five families, comprising 235 people, who have been displaced. Of that 235, 40 people, from nine families, are now living in the Felix Cohen Home for the Elderly; two families, about 17 people, live in Joiner Hall; and the other thirty-four families are living around the country here with friends and relatives. The Red Cross has done a pretty decent job of feeding the families housed here in the two community facilities. We are working on getting some trailers to house some of these people.

In the last two days there has been a very definite shift in attitude among the representatives of the Department of Justice here. This seems to have come from their realization, as I mentioned earlier, that they cannot negotiate with the AIM people in Wounded Knee, and as a result, the responsibility for operations here seems to be shifting from the Civil Rights Division to people in the Criminal Division. Interestingly enough, just today we got word that the attorneys for the Oglala Sioux Tribe, in Washington, will be attempting to have the Justice Department removed from the reservation entirely. I don't know what that will mean if it is successful, and I am not exactly looking forward to it either.

Things seem to be getting a bit rough for the insurgents inside Wounded Knee, despite the smuggled-in food and all of the pillage of surrounding homes and property. One of the men who came out of there talked with one of the young lawyers from the Justice Department recently. He told the lawyer how the insurgents were running short of food and only got one or two meals a day. He himself had been in there about three days and had only two meals. He said that there were some very dedicated people in there, and he left the impression that someone would have to go in and get them out. There was no way they could be negotiated out; they were the type of people who liked firing at the marshals and who made a big deal about being at war.

Today we finished off the material on the enrollment and sent it in. Boy, am I glad that's gone! The final count came out as follows:

Oglala Sioux who are over eighteen years of age as of March 19, 1973:

Resident on the reservation:	5,447
Resident off the reservation:	2,981
Unknown as to address:	1,090
Total	9,518

Of this number, the following are eighteen through twenty years old:

Resident on the reservation:	670
Resident off the reservation:	119
Unknown as to address:	16
Total	805

Louis Bad Wound came to see me again today, representing AIM. He asked me to get the wife of the man who was shot in the head out of jail and get her up to Rapid City to be with her husband in the hospital. I told him I would. When I checked on it, I found that the Department of Justice had already taken care of this. I felt good about the system when I could report back to Louis that this had already been done without any input from me or from AIM.

I got to see a copy of a flier put out by one of the civil rights lawyers in defense of the takeover of Wounded Knee. It sure made me wonder about the people involved in the propaganda wars of this country. It would seem that one truthful statement, or two or three, in the total presentation would have lent credence to the host of untruthful statements. But I could find no truthful statements, nothing accurate in what he said in that flier. I knew about most of what he was saying, and none of it that I had knowledge of was stated correctly. I wondered how many people would take all of that at face value and believe it.

It seems like everyone is being investigated around here. I had a visit today from Jim Wilson, the chairman's brother. He is a brilliant, very astute young man with a Ph.D. who has worked in Washington as head of the Indian desk in the

Office for Equal Opportunity. He quit his job to come out here and write a book on Wounded Knee. He was investigated and questioned by the FBI for supposedly having taken a bribe. The whole thought of Jim Wilson taking a bribe is laughable. It makes me wonder who will be next, who will be the next one questioned and charged with violating someone's civil rights. Dick Wilson has been charged with this, and so have several of the BIA policemen. I just wonder when my turn is coming.

April 22, 1973

Sunday night. The weekend was pretty light as far as I was concerned. I went over to Chadron Saturday and did the laundry. Then I went on down to Fort Robinson to look at the place where Dull Knife and his band of Cheyennes were caught and run down. The final battlefield there is called War Bonnet Battlefield. I wanted to see it but I couldn't find exactly where it was. Some day I will have somebody show me the exact location. As I drove along, I was watching the roads for people who might be coming to the "Woodstock of the North" at Wounded Knee at Easter time. Word is that there will be quite a gathering, but I saw only one carload of people of the kind that you would think would be coming to such a festival, and the Nebraska State Patrol was watching it.

I stayed at home today and worked all day on getting my notes and so forth straightened around. I went over to the office for a while this evening to see what was happening. There was a rumor of another airplane drop. I didn't have time to check this out, but if it is true it will be at least the fourth time supplies have been dropped inside Wounded Knee by airplane. Of course, everyone has been watching the incoming people, hoping to avoid trouble over the intended celebration here over Easter. The government's tactic in this regard seems to have been very successful. The FBI, it seems, has watched these groups as they started out from their various locations all over the country. I don't know how they manage it, but they seem to know who is who and where they all are. If a group is carrying contraband or weapons or things of that kind, the FBI stops them and arrests them as soon as they cross a state line. We haven't had near the influx of people that was expected. About twenty were arrested trying to get into Wounded Knee today. Of course, I don't know how many have gotten in, but a major celebration here has certainly been headed off.

The man wounded in the head is still in critical condition. He is from Cherokee, North Carolina, it seems, and his name is Frank Clearwater. It is incredible to me that we don't know of more casualties from inside Wounded Knee. When you think that 50,000 to 100,000 rounds have been fired in this war, which is now nearly two months old, it seems inevitable that more people than we have heard about have been injured. As I've said before, I wonder where these people are. Why haven't they come out or been evacuated out? The fact that more of the wounded have not come out to receive medical attention speaks for the dedication many of these people must have. Then there is also the remark made by the policeman in our office at the time of the first Wounded Knee agreement, the rumor about the two new graves in the village there. I think I will make a recommendation that once the area is reoccupied, all the surrounding ground should be examined. Otherwise, rumors will be floating around for decades that there are people who died in Wounded Knee and are buried in unknown grave sites. This could lead to another legend like that of Crazy Horse. He was killed at Fort Robinson in 1877, and his body was taken by his family up into the country right north of here. To this day no one has known where he was buried.

April 24, 1973

This entry concerns the events of yesterday—Monday, April 23—and today—Tuesday, April 24. These are indeed trying

times. It all started Monday evening. I was at home, just sitting around visiting after dinner, when I got a phone call in-
forming me that the marshals had just arrested the Indians
manning the citizens' roadblock. I waited around for a while,
figuring that I would soon get more calls and more information, and I did. Bob Ecoffey called and asked me to meet him
in front of the BIA building. I walked over, and there were the
marshals, getting the men from the roadblock ready to go to
Rapid City. They were being handcuffed and fixed so that they
could travel comfortably. Bob Ecoffey, of course, and Dick
Wilson were there. Wilson was standing in the background,
playing it pretty cool. Bob and some of the others from the
roadblock wanted me to stop the whole thing. Of course it
was out of my hands completely; it was in the hands of the
marshals. Bob wanted me to get Del Eastman to stop it, but
of course there was nothing Del could do either against the
United States Marshal Service, and I told Bob this. A group
of people had come along there as well, and it looked like
there was going to be a real confrontation between members
of the Oglala Sioux Tribe and the federal marshals. The folks
were shouting and yelling. Some of those from the roadblock
were shouting at me, "By God, you've got to go tomorrow
morning if you don't stop this!" So now I have another group
that wants me out of here, and these have been my friends up
until now.

Bill Hall, second in command of the marshals at Pine
Ridge, was in charge at the scene, and I suggested that he had
better get his prisoners on the road quickly before he had real
trouble. Then I went into the building, accompanied by Dick
Wilson and four or five others. We went in with the intention
of calling the tribal attorney. We tried and couldn't reach him.
I asked Bill Hall if he could come in and discuss it, and he said
he couldn't, but he suggested that I call Marshal Colburn. I
went upstairs and knocked on the door to the office where
Colburn was closeted with Gary Hageman from the Justice
Department, Criminal Division. Hageman opened the door
about six inches and I told him that I wanted to see Marshal

Colburn. He said that it would be a while, so I asked to have Colburn call me when he got through. I went back downstairs and we tried to call three more attorneys, all related to the tribe, but again we couldn't reach any of them.

Dick Wilson and his group decided to go over to the tribal office and call the newspapers and television stations. This would spread the word that they wanted a couple of hundred people to man that roadblock Tuesday to show the federal Department of Justice that they couldn't do that to them.

After they left, Dwight Mirable and I went back upstairs. The outer door to where Colburn and Hageman were conferring was locked this time, so I knocked and was again told that it would be a while. Dwight and I waited there in the hallway, and after about ten minutes the men from Justice came out. Dwight and I went in, and there were Marshals Colburn, Hall, and Richardson. After a time, Gary Hageman came back too, and Toby Eagle Bull was also there for part of the discussion, at our request. Naturally, we wanted to know what had caused this action on the part of the marshals. What had happened was this: The marshals had gone out to the citizens' roadblock to get the representatives from the Community Relations Service into Wounded Knee. These are people who, as Toby Eagle Bull informed us, are not federal employees but are here under contract to the government. Their purpose is ostensibly to communicate with the people of both sides, but they have endeared themselves to AIM and are disliked by the local people displaced from Wounded Knee. The government wants them treated like part of the Justice Department and insists that they be allowed to enter the occupied area. The tribe and the men on the roadblock do not regard them as such and refused to allow them to pass. The marshals and the men at the roadblock argued over this for a while. Bill Hall said that the discussion was peaceable, but finally it got to the point where the folks on the roadblock said, "If there is going to be bloodshed, let it start here." That was when the marshals arrested them.

Unfortunately, our discussion of the situation degenerated

into a heated argument. Colburn was pushing me to tell him the name of the ex-convict on the roadblock who was not supposed to be carrying a gun. I finally did tell him, but only with the remark, "I probably tell you more than you tell me." Dwight echoed that sentiment with something like "You don't keep us informed." At that, Colburn really blew up. He kept insisting that he did talk to us at the time. He criticized Dwight and the BIA police: said that Dwight didn't know what he was doing, never did anything; as head of the police force, he wasn't doing his job or he would have had the citizens' roadblock out of there already; the BIA police weren't any good, and the marshals couldn't get any support from them. I tried to remind Colburn that the Justice Department were the ones in charge and that we were only auxiliaries in this situation, but he just kept tearing into Dwight. One thing he said that I found interesting was, "You people don't know how close you are to having a trusteeship here, and all of you will be out of a job!"

Finally he broke off the conversation, saying that he was going home and didn't want to hear any more about it that night. We left, stopping to talk to Bill Hall on the way. Bill said that Colburn, and Richardson as well, had had the guns of the citizens' roadblock in their faces more than once and that they were getting tired of it. The roadblock just had to be taken out. He said, "If you folks want to carry this on and fight over it, Colburn will win." We said, "We have no interest in fighting; we just want to do our jobs." "Well, yes, " he said, "we all do. Let's just forget about it and see if we can start over tomorrow." About that time, Colburn came out of the office, shook hands, and apologized for blowing his top. He was carrying a hell of a load, as we all are, and I guess we all should work together a little better.

I went over to Dick Wilson's office, and he had already gone home. I didn't know what was happening on the tribal end of the situation except for what I had told Colburn, namely, that the tribe was gathering its forces together and that the roadblock would be back in force the next day. I went home and went to bed completely beat, wondering and not knowing what to do. For a time I gave up on it and went to sleep. Then, in the middle of the night, around 3:00 A.M., I was awakened by two men at my door. They were from the FBI: big men; middle-aged; physically powerful; powerful, too, in the positions they held. Their visit concerned the lives of people I knew, in situations I could surely understand. They asked, "What can we do?" I responded to their request and rode around with them in that early morning. I wondered whether or not I should wake up Dick Wilson and Bob Ecoffey. I decided not to and decided instead to have a go at it the next day. I went home to sleep for a couple of hours, feeling better because I had a plan.

Fairly early on Tuesday morning, one of the FBI men and I went to Dick Wilson's house. He was just getting up and was sitting there bare chested, drinking a cup of coffee. He had just had an attack of gout and had to use crutches. I talked to him about my plan and got things set up with the tribe. Getting the same thing arranged with the Department of Justice was another matter. What I wanted to do was to get the representatives of the Justice Department and the representatives of the government of the tribe together that afternoon at a meeting at my home. The problem, of course, was that Dick Wilson's forces were gathering together with guns, and the young hotheads in the Justice Department were insisting that there would be no more roadblocks. Dick Hellstern did not want to meet with the tribe, but I finally just insisted.

The meeting at my home broke down completely, and I knew that I had lost it. The collapse came when Dick Hellstern took a real hard line, most of it not in his actual statements but more in his attitude. Suddenly again there was the "buckskin curtain," and all of the tribal representatives—executive committee, business manager, everyone—just walked away. I knew then that unless something was done, there was no way it could end except in armed confrontation between the Justice Department and the people they had been called in to protect. The urgency of the situation called for something I very seldom do. I telephoned direct to Marvin Franklin, assistant secretary of the interior for Indian affairs. My report to him was in two parts: the factual statement of the current situation at Pine Ridge, and the recommendation that he himself come to the reservation immediately. He responded beautifully, no doubt sensing the urgency, and said that he would be there in a matter of hours.

During the day I could not keep track of everything, but the FBI saved it— the same men who had come in the middle of the night. They, of course, were operating under certain restrictions, but they conferred with Acting Director Gray of the FBI, and I had listened to their end of the telephone conversations with him. The end result was that the FBI, who had been directed to maintain responsibility on roadblock 1, quietly extended their jurisdiction down the road just a little bit to include the site of the citizens' roadblock. There the FBI set up their own roadblock and invited the Indians into it. When this happened, I knew that I had won for one day.

Late this afternoon I drove up to Rapid City to meet Assistant Secretary Franklin. We had a drink and a nice dinner and a nice visit at the Elk's Club in Rapid City. Tonight was my first night out in quite a while. I am greatly relieved that I have successfully bought some time and that so far, at least, tragedy has been averted. All day today, I was certain that someone was going to be killed. We were minutes away from it most all of the day. I didn't feel like I was the one who would be killed, like I have felt at certain times this past year, but someone else. I don't know which of these feelings is the worst. In the one, there is a kind of terrible finality to it; you leave the house thinking you will never come back. In the other, it is not so final because you will still be there afterward, but it is awfully hard to take to think that today some of the people you know so well and love so much will be killed.

April 25, 1973

Back in Pine Ridge this morning, I felt better because I now had a bigger man on the scene, someone who could perhaps deal with the Department of Justice from a more authoritative position than I could in my capacity as superintendent. Marvin Franklin is indeed a strong man, and he went to work immediately. His first stop upon arriving in Pine Ridge was with Dick Wilson. I stayed away and let the two of them talk. The tribe was attacking on three levels: First, they were bringing in all of their people to replace those who had been arrested at the citizens' roadblock. Second, they were working through their attorney to be sure the whole thing was legal so that they could not be challenged by the marshals and the Justice Department here. Third, they were attacking at the level of the BIA and the Justice Department in Washington to get an order handed down allowing the citizens' roadblock to remain.

Yesterday, even after I thought the possibility of violence had been forestalled, we came within seconds of disaster over the roadblock. At a press conference yesterday afternoon, the press representatives questioned Dick Hellstern about the Indians they had seen manning the roadblock. Dick Hellstern didn't know what the FBI had done and so he said, "There are no Indians on that roadblock." The press insisted, because they had, of course, seen them. Hellstern was so concerned about this that he left the press conference and went upstairs. When he came back down, he said, "It is an FBI roadblock; it is ours." And of course, it was.

I don't know whether or not Hellstern knew at that point what had happened, but if he didn't know then, he soon found out. The result was that Hellstern and Kent Frizzell and Marshal Colburn went out to the new FBI roadblock being manned by Wilson's Indians. I had already left by this time to go to Rapid City. When they arrived at the roadblock they were met by a seventeen- or eighteen-year-old Indian boy armed with a double-barreled shotgun. He rapped on the windows of the car and said, "Roll down the window." Here were individuals of authority and responsibility, men accustomed to giving orders and making challenges; now they were being inspected and challenged themselves. The marshal bounded out of the car with what some said was an M-1 carbine, others an M-16. The marshal with his rifle and the Indian kid with his shotgun faced each other at gunpoint. The kid was scared and shaky, and I found out later that that shotgun had a hair trigger. One of those shakes could have touched it off, and that would have been it: two dead, a teenage boy and the director of the U.S. Marshals. A quick-thinking young man from the FBI stepped in between them and asked them both to lower their guns. The kid had guts. He said, "I will lower mine when he lowers his." So Colburn did; he put his weapon away, and once again tragedy was averted.

Confrontations of this sort could not be allowed to continue. This had to be resolved and quickly. Marvin Franklin had arranged a meeting for three o'clock in the afternoon. It was to include the Justice representatives, the FBI, the marshals, the BIA, and the tribe. I had heard a little bit about this meeting, and Wyman Babby and I were going over to talk to Dick Wilson about it. Franklin told us not to talk to Dick about the meeting. "I will be running the meeting this afternoon," he said, "and I don't want anyone coming into it with any preconceived notions." We did what he asked. The subject of the meeting did come up in our discussion with the chairman, but we dutifully skirted it.

At the meeting I was very, very impressed with Franklin. He is not a particularly eloquent man in quick give-and-take conversation, but he was certainly eloquent today. He did an excellent job of presenting the feelings that Indians have toward the entire federal establishment. He explained how Indians generally do not see much difference between the FBI, the marshals, the BIA, and so forth because each one of them represents the federal government. For that reason, dealing with one is like dealing with them all. Franklin made a plea for unity in a most quiet, eloquent fashion. I sat and looked again at the faces of the FBI men, the marshals and their chief marshal, and the Justice people, and I could see that they were as impressed as I was.

To solve the problem of the roadblock, Franklin proposed something that we had used back in November of 1972, at the time of the first AIM intrusion. This was an auxiliary police force composed of members of the tribe and operating under the supervision of the professional law-enforcement bodies here. This same plan had been implemented by Dick Wilson, Wyman Babby, and me in 1972, and it had worked well. It had not worked well in the beginning of the present confrontation because I lost control of it. On the insistence of the federal establishment, with the concurrence of the BIA area director, it was phased out. Now here was the same program again: an auxiliary police force. It was interesting to watch the marshals and the FBI react to this. They were willing to help; they were willing to give training; but even with that training, they were not willing to let these individuals act in an armed law-enforcement capacity alongside them. Then Franklin suggested that perhaps the Indians could be used as an intelligence force. The marshals and the FBI responded quickly to this because they could see this as a way out. The Indians would be only a supportive force and would not be armed. The feds would be in control.

Among the issues discussed at the meeting was general strategy for confronting the Wounded Knee occupation force. Kent Frizzell was recently confirmed as a chief solicitor of the Department of the Interior, but since he has been the chief negotiator for the Department of Justice for these many days, he was still wearing the Justice hat in this meeting. He stated three alternatives for dealing with the situation: One was simply to walk away; this was unacceptable for many reasons and unavailable at this time because it would require approval of the White House. A second was to go in and forcibly reoccupy the area; again this was unacceptable and again un-available because it required White House approval also. The third was to maintain a perimeter and try to negotiate, the exact procedure followed for nearly sixty days now. Jim Wil-son, the chairman's brother, was at the meeting, and he was quizzing Frizzell as to who was ultimately in charge here. Frizzell tried to evade the issue and did so pretty successfully, but Jim Wilson probed and probed, and finally it was admitted that the authority here was the attorney general of the United States. Yet, unsaid in all of this was the knowledge that the decisions were really being made by the White House staff.

Pete Swift Bird gave a most insightful and surprising characterization of the situation inside Wounded Knee. He seemed to know more about what was going on in there than the marshals did, and I could see the discomfiture of the marshals as he was recounting the details. Evidently, Pete Swift Bird had been in Wounded Knee himself; he had to have been inside to possess the knowledge he displayed today. At any rate, he talked of leadership problems among the AIM people in Wounded Knee. He said that one leader—Dennis Banks, I believe—had been firmly in control but that two more leaders were now struggling for position against him. His description of the breakdown in authority there was very interesting.

The discussion then turned to the issue of communication. This is, in my opinion, where the Justice Department really misses it. They seem to have no idea of some of the basic prin-ciples of negotiation and problem solving. We in the BIA take the approach of involving as many people as we possibly can on a level equal to ourselves. I call it the philosophy of equal experts. The Justice Department, on the other hand, as I have said so often, relates only upward, not laterally. It seems to be completely foreign to them to think that they could gain knowledge or help in making a decision from anyone in the BIA or in the Oglala Sioux Tribe. They make their decisions and then just tell us what they are doing. Hellstern again restated his position in this regard very strongly and in a fashion that really turned people off. He said, in essence, "*We* are going to have control; *we* will make the decisions; let there be no question about it." The meeting broke up with not a great deal being resolved, but another meeting was scheduled for tomorrow morning at eleven o'clock.

Another major event of the day concerned a protest march in support of the insurgents at Wounded Knee. We did not get to pay much attention to it today because we were so busy with other things. If it hadn't been for the explosive situation over the roadblock, the protest march would have been a major crisis. As it was, the law-enforcement agencies handled it exceptionally well and without incident. About seventy demonstrators, led by Vernon Bellecourt, were walking from Crow Dog Park, on the Rosebud Reservation, to Wounded Knee. Their destination was changed to Kyle in the middle of their walk. Most of the group were young whites, along with a black or two, some Chicanos, and a few Indians. I never did see these marchers myself, but I received pretty good reports on them.

The decision to move the protesters outside the boundaries of the reservation had been made a couple of days before, but the tactical decision as to exactly when this should be done was left to Del Eastman. He determined that it would be this morning. As the group continued their march toward Kyle, they encountered a line of BIA policemen blocking the road ahead of them. Del Eastman's team of about sixty BIA police was backed up by about fifteen FBI agents and an FBI helicopter and by five marshals who could act as a specialty gas team if necessary. They served the Oglala Sioux Tribal Court exclusion order, that is, the one barring nonresidents from the reservation. The group chose not to resist the police line, and even Vernon Bellecourt, who is generally very vocal, kept pretty quiet this time for fear of being arrested. The group turned back and no arrests were made. It is significant that the FBI was acting in this instance in full support of the BIA police in enforcing a court order of the Oglala Sioux Tribe.

Meanwhile, the war at Wounded Knee went on. Frank

Clearwater, the man who was wounded in the head last week, died today at the hospital in Rapid City. Marshal Colburn had predicted days ago that if he died, there would be an effort to bury him at Wounded Knee. This is, in fact, what is happening. The people of Wounded Knee today sent a message to the Justice Department by means of the radio which had been supplied to them by the marshals. The message was, "We will donate a part of our ground as a burial place for those of us who will be massacred at Wounded Knee." They also proclaimed four days of mourning for the man who has died and a four-day moratorium on negotiations. The tribal court has said that under no circumstances will this foreigner be allowed to be buried on the reservation, for despite his Indian name, we know that this man is not an Indian, at least not any more than any of the rest of us whose ancestors have been in this country for a long time and cannot be directly traced. But somewhere along the line, he identified himself as Indian, came to Wounded Knee in support of AIM; and now he is dead. I wonder if this man, who was a nonentity to most of us up until a few days ago, will now become a martyr for the AIM cause.

In the midst of everything today, two old Indian ladies came into the BIA office with one of those old traditional problems. They told how they had come before and had been turned away because people were there with guns. Today they did get in, and they came to me. I worked very hard on their problem, and it felt good to be helpful to someone again.

Also, today was the day I first found out for sure that the entire cost of this operation in response to the Wounded Knee takeover is going to be footed by the BIA. It must be around three million dollars by now, with no end in sight. The direct cost to the BIA at Pine Ridge in terms of lost wastebaskets, damaged typewriters, trampled lawns, blown-up bridges, damaged roads, and lost time of employees is well over a half million dollars. Besides this monetary loss to the Pine Ridge Agency, over twenty thousand child-days of school have been lost up to this point, and the seeds of hate for another hundred years have been sown.

At the end of the day, I accompanied Marvin Franklin up to Hot Springs, where he was staying. At his invitation Wyman Babby and I had a drink with him in his hotel room and a nice dinner at the country club. No formal meeting, just a re-cap and evaluation of the day's events. At the country club, I saw a lot of the FBI men who have been working regularly at Pine Ridge. These are the agents who regularly oppose the in-surgents at Wounded Knee in the day-by-day confrontations. I couldn't help but think how different their lot is in this conflict from that of the opposition. Tonight those people at Wounded Knee are surely cold and hungry. Again tomorrow, they will face the terrible challenge of attacking the might and power and inertia of the United States government. And yet they continue.

April 26, 1973

I felt much more optimistic this morning. At least we made it through the last two days. The time that we were able to buy to get Franklin up here has made all the difference. After having a good steak dinner and visit with us at the country club at Hot Springs, Franklin stayed awake part of the night thinking and putting things together. Then, on the way down from Hot Springs, he wrote out a program. He showed it to Wyman Babby and me, and we both made a comment or two. Franklin rewrote it and then went into the eleven o'clock meeting and sold it.

Again Hellstern was the stumbling block. Gerald Ge-reau, who has been here gathering information for Senator Henry M. Jackson's Senate committee, conducted part of the meeting, and his authority to do so was challenged by Hell-stern. Hellstern's attitude turned Franklin off and Dick Wil-son as well, and I feared for a time that it was all going to

fall apart. The meeting broke up and reconvened in the afternoon. The third time was the charm: this time we had an
agreement. Franklin did what I'm sure I could never have
done: he herded that bunch of mavericks right into the corral
like a cowboy with a trained cow horse. He ended up putting
together the kind of arrangement that can work among the
various agencies and jurisdictions represented here. It can
work, that is, if each of us is willing to work at it, and at the
moment, I think we all are.

The terms of the agreement are these: the Justice Department will not negotiate on anything relating to tribal sovereignty without tribal presence. The Justice Department will
consult with the tribe at all times and in everything, steadily
and consistently. About forty Oglala Sioux will be trained by
the Marshal Service and the FBI to be incorporated into the
federal effort to contain the situation at Wounded Knee; each
one of these trained individuals will be operating under the
direction of one of four agencies—the Border Patrol, the U.S.
Marshal Service, the FBI, or the BIA police.

During the past couple of days, then, the major portion of
the time of many very high-paid men has been devoted to the
project of settling the differences between the various organizations which are presumably working together here. The
problem brought us close to death, seconds away, on more
than one occasion. And through it all, the cool one was the
tribal president, Dick Wilson. He played it beautifully: calm,
purposeful, giving in on the little things while maintaining
his position on the big things. The stars of the situation, as far
as I am concerned, were the men of the FBI, the BIA, and the
tribal leadership. These were the ones who best maintained
their equilibrium in the face of enormous pressures.

The group of marchers who were turned back yesterday
at the east line of the reservation sneaked back in. They got
over to Kyle last night, and about ten o'clock, a large group of
them were arrested: fifty-seven individuals, fourteen of them
Indians, the rest non-Indians. There they were, fifty-seven of
them, in a jail that would have been crowded with twenty.

The FBI interviewed each one of them to see if there were any federal offenses against them. The FBI did take a few for such charges, but the rest were turned over to the tribe to face charges of "disobedience to the lawful order of the Oglala Sioux Tribal Court." The significant thing about this is that an Indian tribe is here exercising jurisdiction over non-Indians who have come onto its reservation. This action is very likely to be challenged in the courts, because nowhere in this country does a non-Indian come under the jurisdiction of an Indian court. (This concerns only misdemeanors, of course, not major crimes, which are all strictly federal offenses.) I don't know whether or not we would win such a challenge in court, but if we do win, it will represent a giant step forward in terms of Indian sovereignty.

Related to this question of jurisdiction was the situation yesterday morning when Del Eastman served the tribal court order on the marchers. His roadblock was set up in Bennett County, and there is considerable controversy over which body exercises jurisdiction in Bennett County: the State of South Dakota or the Oglala Sioux Tribe and the BIA. Del was really smart in the way he handled this, I think. He did something I would not have thought of. When he sent his troops out to set up the roadblock, he stopped at the courthouse in Martin to see the state attorney. What Del said, in essence, was this: "We are going to remove these people from Bennett County. We know that there is a controversy over what the jurisdiction is, but we are now assuming that jurisdiction. We know that you want these people removed as much as we do, and so we are going to remove them." The attorney, naturally, said that he could not accept or agree to that. Del said, "I know you can't, and I don't expect you to. However, I don't have much time, so we *are* assuming jurisdiction, and I am leaving now to take these people off." So that is how the BIA police came to operate in white-dominated Martin. We may hear more about this one.

The firing on the perimeter continued today. The insurgents were firing on the government bunkers, and in response, the order was given to use a nontoxic gas. These kinds of decisions cannot be handed down hastily. In this case the government roadblock way out at Wounded Knee, seventeen miles from Pine Ridge, radioed the command post in the BIA building. Two marshals then rushed from the BIA building to the tribal building, where Wayne Colburn was in the meeting with Marvin Franklin and all the rest of us. Colburn was all business and efficiency in handling the problem. He quickly gave the order to use a chemical agent. The command post informed the insurgents by radio of the order to use gas, and the question came back from Wounded Knee, "Does this mean that you are going to fire one for one on us, or are you going to make a massive attack?" The marshal on the radio had to laugh when he heard this; he just couldn't believe it. His reply was very circumspect: "We are not going to reveal our battle plans." I don't think there was much more firing, if any, after that.

There was an AIM meeting, or rally, today at Kyle. Frank Fools Crow had advertised it in a flier, asking for all Sioux to come and join in support of the Oglala. There were about a hundred people at the rally. Kent Frizzell went out there to check things out. He was worried about the legality of the exclusion order of the tribal court. We had, of course, discussed this very court order about three weeks ago at the briefing meetings, but he had not seen the significance of it until he got out there and faced the people coming into Kyle, gathering for the AIM meeting. Del Eastman had two police units sitting at the reservation line waiting for the Reverend Charles Abernathy. Their intention was that if he came from inside the reservation he would be escorted off, and if he came from the outside he would be turned back. Frizzell thought that this was a bad move, and on his recommendation it was agreed that the good reverend would be allowed to meet with the group and that papers would be served on him after he left. Again, I suspect that we will have a lot of trouble over this one tomorrow.

Marvin Franklin left Pine Ridge this evening, having

achieved some kind of order and agreement. He is going to Oklahoma, where AIM has decided not to have their annual convention. It looks like Rosebud, South Dakota, may have won the prize instead. If so, we will be in action up here for quite a while. In any event, as of this moment it seems like we are in better shape than we were, and it can be characterized, I think, in this way: Dick Hellstern, a key figure in the Justice Department for maybe forty-five days now, for the first time referred to Dick Wilson as "Chairman Wilson" instead of "Chief Wilson."

May 1, 1973

Much has happened since my last entry, on Thursday night. No longer can we say that we have gotten by without anyone on the reservation being killed. Our second known death at Wounded Knee came Friday afternoon, April 27. It was Lawrence Lamont, Jr., called Buddy, age thirty-one, a local Oglala. His mother, Agnes Lamont, is a matron, or teacher's aide, for the BIA. Buddy was one of nine children and the only son in the family. He was Toby Eagle Bull's brother-in-law.

A terrible afternoon for everyone: the first reports, the hurry of identification, the growing chill of realization, the first known death of an Oglala close to home. The family—grief-stricken, angry, outraged—blames the BIA: he was shot in the back by BIA policemen, they say. Others blame AIM: he was shot in the back by AIM to create a martyr.

Buddy's sister Rose Peoples, who was in Wounded Knee as well, came out with him in the ambulance. We found out that she has a tiny baby, born two weeks ago in Wounded Knee. The baby wasn't with her when she came out. We wonder who is caring for it inside the AIM fortress.

Toby Eagle Bull came to see me that afternoon in my office. We didn't say hardly anything. He just sat for quite a while, not wanting to go home. He said, "Last night the dogs were howling. They woke us up. It went on for ten minutes, and we couldn't quiet them. I told my wife that something was going to happen. We believe that, we Indians." He sat there with me a while longer, not saying any more. Finally he rose and said, "Just as well face it now." I watched him as he walked out across the agency lawn. He was tired, troubled; his shoulders sagged. I called him several times later in the evening. He was okay. And it was too quiet all the rest of the night.

Saturday and Sunday were completely full days. Most of my time was spent working with Kent Frizzell, who was trying to head off a confrontation on the Clearwater burial. As I said before, Frank Clearwater, poor man, had decided somewhere along the line that he was an Indian, although he is not enrolled in any tribe. His service record lists his name as Clear and his ancestry as Irish. His wife, Morning Star Clearwater, and his mother wanted him buried at Wounded Knee, but the executive committee and the Oglala Sioux Tribal Court both said no and issued a court order to that effect. When asked what AIM intended to do in the face of the court order, Russell Means said that if Clearwater were to be stopped at the reservation line, he would be buried right in the middle of the road! We were at an impasse.

Kent Frizzell finally got an idea from Leonard Crow Dog, one of the signatories of the first Wounded Knee agreement. Crow Dog is a Rosebud Sioux. He suggested that Clearwater could be buried at his place on the Rosebud Reservation, but they wanted to hold a night of wake for him at Frank Fools Crow's place, which is over by Kyle on the Pine Ridge Reservation. Frizzell agreed to this, and now something had to be done about the court order against Clearwater's being brought onto Pine Ridge. I went to work on that end of it Sunday night, April 29. I got hold of Emma Nelson, the treasurer of the tribal executive committee, and Dick Wilson, the chairman, and cleared it with both of them. Then, the first thing Monday morning, we met with Judge Tibbits and petitioned him to amend his order. He did so, and the way was cleared for the wake at Fools Crow's. In the meantime, we had not reached Toby Eagle Bull, the secretary of the executive committee; and when we did contact him, he was not in agreement. In fact, he was angry. He said that we couldn't negotiate with AIM and expect them to keep their part of the bargain. If Clearwater were allowed to enter the reservation, he said, he would very likely remain here.

On Monday, April 30, the Clearwater procession was escorted into the reservation by police. There were about ten carloads of sympathizers who accompanied the hearse, and they all stayed overnight at Fools Crow's. Then, this morning, Del Eastman and the BIA police, with U.S. Marshals and FBI agents in support, escorted the procession to Rosebud. In the meantime, the tribal officials at Rosebud had become aware of the whole situation and had decided that they didn't want Clearwater at Rosebud, either. The Rosebud Tribal Council passed a resolution to prevent his being buried on the Rosebud Reservation and were in the process of having a court order issued to that effect.

When the Clearwater procession reached the line between Pine Ridge and Rosebud, Del Eastman was met by Lou White, special officer from Rosebud. White was waiting for the Rosebud court order, which hadn't arrived yet, and had sent a tribal police car down to Crow Dog's place to keep the mourners away from there too. Del's instructions from me were to take the body north into Pennington County or Jackson County if there was, in fact, a court order against their proceeding into Rosebud. The procession was stopped at the border while Del Eastman and Lou White were conferring. Along came Vernon Bellecourt, and after some argument he got in the hearse and pushed the driver aside. He took off with the hearse, drove by the police car, and went on into Crow Dog's. A confrontation there seemed inevitable, until Lou White began working on a compromise solution that would be acceptable to the tribal council, the tribal court, and the people of Rosebud.

Judy Cornelius, the sister of our secretary, Jo, and a reporter for the *Oglala Sioux Nation News*, was there at Rosebud when the council met. There was a white man there, she said, who was reminding the council that Indians have respect for the dead and that they should allow this man to be buried on the reservation. Webster Two Hawk, chairman of the Rosebud council, countered with the statement that Indians always go home to be buried, implying that this white man with an Indian name should go to his own home. Then he said in Sioux to the council something to the effect that "We don't want this scraggly white man telling us what to do." Finally a compromise was reached, and Frank Clearwater was buried in a white man's cemetery on the Rosebud Reservation. What a sad thing for the man and his family, not to have a place to be buried.

Gerry Gereau, as I've said, has been here representing Senator Henry Jackson for the Senate Interior Affairs Committee. He likes to feel right in the middle of things, and he certainly ended up in the thick of it the other day. He was driving around the country looking things over, when he met a friend of his from a previous time stopped on the road with a flat tire. The friend was a marshal, on his way to his roadblock duty station, so Gerry gave him a lift. Once at the roadblock, Gerry was pinned down there for five hours because of the firing. He took two hours of tape of the action, which he sent in to the Senate subcommittee to give them a real idea of the situation here. He also talked to Frank Fools Crow and other AIM members. He took statements of all kinds on tape. I myself gave him a written statement. All this will be used at the Senate subcommittee hearings, which will be held shortly. Gereau left yesterday evening, and I think we made a pretty good impression.

Yesterday, Monday, Marvin Franklin's plan began to be put into operation among "the allies," that is, the Justice Department, the BIA, and the Oglala Sioux Tribe. Yesterday, for the first time, Dick Wilson was included in the regular morning briefing sessions, and he will be from now on. The meetings are supposed to be held at the same time every day now, 9:00 or 9:30 A.M. Also, today, we got started on the training for the auxiliary police force. About sixteen Oglalas were hired into the Marshal Service on a BIA contract. They were hired on as GS-4's, although they were supposed to be only GS-3's. Dick Wilson and I had a hassle over that one, and he won out for the higher grade. Tribal chairmen usually do win. It will cause us a little trouble, but we will cross that bridge when we come to it.

Wyman Babby called me tonight with something kind of ominous sounding. He said that someone—he wouldn't specify who—was after Dick Wilson, and he felt that Dick should leave town for two or three weeks. He wanted me to tell Dick to be very careful about where he goes and who he has around him. He said he couldn't say more than that. Anyway, Dick Wilson is wearing a gun, as he has since early in this conflict. I never thought I would see the chairman of any tribe wearing a gun!

May 3, 1973

Yesterday morning, May 2, began with an interview with Ethel Merrival. Ethel is one of the mixed-bloods on the reservation and is very active in tribal affairs. I knew her twenty years ago when I first came to Pine Ridge. Ethel is one of the tribal lawyers and has quite a bit to do with the court. She is definitely an AIM supporter and admits to being one but insists that she does not believe in violence. She had quite a few complaints when she talked to me today, mainly concerning law enforcement here on the reservation. She mentioned particular officers who she felt were not doing their duty or were using improper procedures. She mentioned several incidents which she thought had not been investigated seriously or dealt with correctly. She was very angry at Judge Dorothy Richards, who tried the case of Officer Glen Three Stars. He was the one who was arrested back on April 6 for assaulting Hobart Keith. Hobart Keith, incidentally, is Ethel Merrival's brother. Judge Richards gave Glen a fine of five cents and a sentence of ten minutes in jail. Ethel was incensed and told Mrs. Richards that this was a mockery of justice. The judge replied that she had just made the punishment fit the crime. One thing that Ethel complained about will have to be looked into seriously. She claimed that there is unequal application of the law on the reservation to mixed-bloods and full-bloods. She said that when a full-blood has a complaint against him, it is served at once, whereas a mixed-blood with a complaint against him is not too likely to be served. I asked Mike Windham, area special officer, to compile a list of the people arrested in January of 1972 and in January of 1973 to see whether or not there were in fact more full-bloods arrested than mixed-bloods.

Shortly after Ethel's visit, the nine-thirty briefing meeting began. In the three days that these joint meetings have been going on now, I have noticed a very definite change in tone and atmosphere. Previously, when the meetings involved just representatives of the Department of Justice and the Department of the Interior, they were deadly serious. In fact, once I had tried to make a joke of something and it had not been appreciated at all. Now everything that happened seemed to be funny, and there was a lot of wisecracking, some of it in poor taste. I get the impression that now that representatives of the tribe are present, none of the vital information is coming out. All of the real business is being taken care of among themselves, behind closed doors or on the phone.

Still, despite the changed character of the meeting, some interesting things were brought up. Dick Heldt, FBI special agent in charge, reported that the Rapid City AIM is full of dissension. The FBI is getting word from its sources in Wounded Knee that Wounded Knee is not getting any support out of Rapid City.

Kent Frizzell mentioned that Leonard Crow Dog accompanied three FBI agents into Wounded Knee to show them the reported new graves down there. The thought was expressed that perhaps these supposed graves could be abandoned bunkers. Shortly after Lamont's death, a cease-fire had been agreed upon, and part of the agreement was a news blackout. It was AIM, in fact, who had asked for the news blackout. The government complied and did not put out any information. As it turned out, AIM wanted to stop all press releases because the press coverage was beginning to favor the federal position. AIM lives on good press coverage even as it lives on food. Once the blackout was in force, AIM began a propaganda campaign all over the country: the Eighty-second Airborne was ready to move in; there were tanks in the area; federal leaflets would be dropped; gas would be dispersed by helicopter; negotiations had ceased. Not about to let AIM win a huge propaganda victory, the government rescinded its promise not to have any press coverage.

A while after the meeting, I left to go up to Cedar Pass to the school board meeting. Afterward I went on to Rapid City, accompanied by a couple of colleagues in the BIA. We had dinner at the officer's club at the air base there. I stayed the night in Rapid City and slept until nearly noon today. I was getting to the point where I had to have some rest. The last few days especially have been terribly trying.

In the hotel dining room at lunch, I ran into Don Loudner, a delightful fellow. He is a Crow Creek Indian and is the governor's commissioner for Indian affairs. He is also a sergeant in the National Guard. After lunch he took me to the yard of the National Guard where the artillery was parked and showed me the infamous "tank." About three days ago a newspaper reporter took a picture of what appeared to be a tank on the Pine Ridge Reservation. The photograph was sent out on the wire services with the report that the United States government was bringing in tanks to clean out the people at Wounded Knee. Well, Kent Frizzell just went crazy. He said that they would have to show him that tank; he would have to go out by helicopter himself and look at it because he knew that there were no U.S. Army tanks in Pine Ridge. They did show him, and there it was: a tank. The Justice Department got stirring around and finally found out that the National Guard had been practicing on their artillery range up near the north edge of the reservation. What the newspaperman had photographed was not a tank, but a 155-mm self-propelled howitzer, the very one that Don Loudner showed me. I had never seen one of these before, not even in a picture, and it really did look like a tank.

After lunch I came on back to Pine Ridge and got to the office about a quarter of four. The place was a madhouse: telephone calls, news conferences, visits with the press, all kinds of things going on. Bob Farring, who was here from the BIA to gather information for Assistant Secretary of the Interior Bill Rogers, has been replaced by a fellow named Bud Shappard. As I said, people keep getting rotated in and out of here. Hardly anyone has been here through the entire siege. In the beginning Bill Rogers had asked me to report to him, and I did try, but he needed more information than I had time to supply him on a regular basis. So he sent Bob Farring to do the job, as I've said, and now Bud Shappard. Both have done an excellent job. The assistant secretary told Bud to overreport rather than underreport, so they have conferred by telephone five different times today, and Bud was trying to call him again as I left the office this evening. I can see why the assistant secretary thought he wasn't being kept abreast of things when I was reporting to him once every two or three days!

I came home tonight and watched the baseball game on television. I was interrupted only twice for phone calls. Maybe things are a little easier than they have been—I don't know—but they can break out again at any minute. Over two months now, two known dead, millions of dollars spent, and still the government keeps negotiating. I suppose after what has happened to them with Watergate, they cannot afford another scandal. And of course people are saying that an Indian reservation is the only place where this kind of destruction would be tolerated. For instance, if AIM had tried to occupy the South Dakota town of Custer rather than stopping at the hit-and-run tactic they did use there, I am sure that the National Guard would have been sent in and AIM would have been dealt with in a very forceful and summary fashion. When it is Indian business, though, they seem to be able to get away with anything.

May 6, 1973

This is the day of the second Wounded Knee agreement, just a month after the first abortive attempt to resolve this conflict. The laying down of arms by the insurgents in Wounded Knee will occur at 7:00 A.M. on Wednesday, May 9. The terms of this agreement are essentially the same as those of the previous one, but if anything, this one is a little bit tougher. It provides for a residual force of United States Marshals to remain in Wounded Knee, and the terms for the laying down of arms are more specific. As before, arrests will be made of those who have federal warrants outstanding against them. Also to be arrested are those who may be indicted by the grand jury between now and Wednesday. Anyone who doesn't fall into one of these two categories will be allowed to leave when the town is reoccupied. The perimeter will be strengthened to prevent people from avoiding arrest by coming out before then. The government, for its part, made three concessions: first, all armored personnel carriers will be withdrawn prior to the laying down of arms; second, one of the chiefs or headmen will be allowed to sit in each bunker occupied by the FBI and the marshals; third, weapons of a "noncombatant nature" may be claimed by the owners and may be returned to them after twenty-four hours.

Some of the signatures on this second agreement are the same as on the first agreement, but there are also some changes.

Crow Dog: He was there last time. As I've mentioned before, he is a Rosebud Sioux.

Frank Kills Enemy: An unusual man, a man of vision—some would say hallucination. Only a few months ago he stood in my office and, looking upward, with a vision upon him, told of the fire and flood and trouble that would come to Pine Ridge and Rapid City. His political position is well known; he has explained it to me many times, and he never moves from it: he rests on treaty law and, accordingly, would have every single individual who has a white ancestor anywhere expelled from the reservation. He can cite a place in the treaty where it says this is exactly what the superintendent is supposed to do.

Matthew H. King: I have never met him, and so I personally don't know much about him. Some of my friends in tribal government identify him as "the mean one of the bunch," one who has had a great influence over the Oglalas in Wounded Knee. He hates tribal government and hates anything connected with the BIA.

Frank Fools Crow: As I've said before, a medicine man, now recognized by the Justice representatives as a headman or chief.

Eugene White Hawk: He is one of those who came to my office the day before all this started and said, with hate, perhaps, but in a controlled, emotionless way, "Why don't you leave here?"

Edward White Dress: I don't know him.

Gladys Bissonette: She signed the first agreement as well.

Roger Iron Cloud: A new name on this second agreement.

Vern Long: The son of Dave Long, who is vice president of the Oglala Sioux Tribe.

Francis Mesteth: Another local Oglala.

Contrary to the previous agreement, all of the signatories of this agreement are local Oglalas, with the exception of Crow Dog.

At the regular briefing meeting this morning, many people were quite jubilant, seeing this agreement as a definite end of the siege. Those of us who have been through the first one were more reserved. Even Kent Frizzell admitted that he has little faith in this agreement coming off, except that maybe the insurgents are more willing now than they were before to resolve the conflict. AIM leader Dennis Banks is now saying,

"We have accomplished what we came here to do, so now we will quit." Still, their past actions have demonstrated that these people cannot be counted on to keep their word.

At a press conference this afternoon, Ramon Roubideaux, chief counsel for AIM, summarized the position of the insurgents: The forthcoming laying down of arms, he said, is both historic and tragic in its implications. Two are dead, and scores are wounded. The people in Wounded Knee are afraid that if they lay down their arms they will be massacred. For this reason they want chiefs or headmen in each bunker, and they want the people from the Community Relations Service to participate in the laying down of arms. The people at Wounded Knee do not have enough bail bond, so AIM is working hard on that. Only Crow Dog has signed the agreement as a representative of AIM; all the rest are local Oglalas.

Roubideaux continued: Situations exist that must be corrected; AIM calls for the reform of existing structures of government. Wounded Knee is a warning; there will be more unless the government changes its system. The Indian Reorganization Act [IRA] is a tragic failure, he claimed; it is not responsive to Indians. Congress must repeal the IRA and allow Indians to go back to the Indian system. These oppressed people will not live under this form of government: they would rather die. There is no communication with Indians by the government; we need a forum in which the Indians can voice their concerns and complaints.

Roubideaux concluded: The AIM objectives at Wounded Knee have been met; sixty-four tribes were represented at Wounded Knee, and this is evidence of widespread dissatisfaction with the BIA. His staff will be working many months into the future to begin fourteen different legal actions. Men cannot be entrusted with too much power. The people must speak.

The significant part of Roubideaux's statement, as I interpreted it, is the call for "reform of existing structures of government." Always before, it has been a question of the dissolution of government. This constitutes some progress,

I suppose, toward reaching a real solution to the deep-seated problems that underlie this whole controversy.

Dick Hellstern made the very good point that if there were to be any more Wounded Knees in the future, things would likely be handled much differently than they were here. Law enforcement, he said, cannot have its posture governed by those who take up arms. Marshal Colburn said that Wounded Knee has been one of the most challenging problems the Justice Department has ever faced, and one of the most difficult aspects of it has been coping with all the various forces here: the community, the citizens' roadblock, the Oglala Sioux tribal government and court, the Oglala Sioux Civil Rights Organization, AIM itself, and others.

After the press conference, I had a flurry of telephone calls from Gerald Gereau, Bill Rogers, Marvin Franklin, and others. It was difficult to call out because the circuits were busy about half the time. I know it was difficult to call in as well, for the same reason. I think every agency represented here was on the phone at the same time. With Franklin I talked about plans for reoccupation and about special assignments of individuals in that operation. Franklin was comprehensive, all-inclusive, in his ability to marshal the forces of the federal government and focus them on the reconstruction that must be done at Wounded Knee. He said, "We'll give you what is needed to put it back together. You have the same coordination you had before."

It was mentioned in the press conference that there seem to be fewer of the diehards, the really dedicated ones, left inside Wounded Knee now than there were at the time of the first agreement. Where did they all go? Perhaps they have been sneaking out, like those Mike Windham reported on this afternoon. Three individuals armed with machine guns sneaked out today, captured a rancher at gunpoint, stole his pickup truck, and escaped. We are looking for them now. I am sure there will be a lot more of this sort of thing between now and Wednesday morning.

May 8, 1973

The timetable for the reoccupation was advanced by twenty-four hours at the request of AIM—specifically, Crow Dog, who came out yesterday, Monday, and surrendered to a federal roadblock, and Dennis Banks, who remained inside. The Justice Department agreed, and the laying down of arms was rescheduled for Tuesday, May 8, at 7:00 A.M.

A major complication in the preparations for the reoccupation concerned the petition of CBS. A few days ago CBS had sent a crew into Wounded Knee, in violation of the restrictions of the Justice Department and the Oglala Sioux tribal court. When they came out they were escorted off the reservation, and CBS was told that they could not come back. Then yesterday, when they saw it all coming to an end, they started putting on the pressure to get back in. They weren't about to miss the reoccupation of Wounded Knee. CBS is apparently very powerful and did their telephoning in all the right places. By Monday evening, top men from CBS were in Rapid City and others were flying in from Denver, and they were still making telephone calls. They couldn't understand what the problem was. To them the exclusion order of the Oglala Sioux tribal court represented no obstacle at all; after all, they said, can't the BIA and the Department of Interior tell the tribe what to do?

The result was that all day yesterday Kent Frizzell was being pressured by the White House to see to it that CBS would not be kept out of Wounded Knee today. It looked like the weight of the Departments of Justice and the Interior, of Kleindienst, Morton, and the White House, would fall on Tribal Judge Dorothy Richards, since she was the one who was first approached about CBS's petition. She declined to hear their petition yesterday because she was at a wake for her cousin. She agreed to hear their petition today, at two o'clock in the afternoon, but she stated that she would have to hear the tribal executive committee's side of the matter as well. Of course, Tuesday afternoon would be too late, and the pressure then fell on me to find a way out. Of course, the issue at stake here was not the filming of the reoccupation but rather the question of tribal sovereignty and the enforcement of orders of the tribal court.

Besides Judge Richards, there are two other tribal judges. The chief judge, Judge Tibbits, lives way out in the country, so we decided to contact Judge Two Bulls, who normally handles juvenile cases and so forth. It was after midnight Monday night when Del Eastman and I left Pine Ridge for Judge Two Bulls's place, which is out in the country a little to the north and west of Oglala. The judge was a bit apprehensive, I think, at receiving a knock on the door at that hour of the night. He recognized us and trusted us, but he was naturally reluctant to come out at that hour. By the time we had delivered our message and started back, it was 1:30 A.M. I was pretty tired when we got back. During the long evening, as we were watching and working, I had watched Kent Frizzell. He too was looking tired, desperately tired. He is a good-looking man, very forceful, very young-looking, normally. But last night I could see around his eyes that the pressure was getting to him.

We both had to be at the office very early this morning, Tuesday, May 8, to meet with CBS. So after a few hours' sleep we both were back. Frizzell had earlier remarked that under no circumstances would he allow the Nixon administration to be embarrassed by CBS on tonight's six o'clock news. This morning Frizzell asked me to call in Del Eastman and order him not to arrest the CBS crew. I declined to give the order to Del: it would have shattered me, and Del as well, if after weeks and months of struggling to uphold tribal government, the order was now given *not* to uphold it.

Frizzell then went to Judge Tibbits. He had asked me beforehand how he should approach the judge, and I advised,

"Just face him with everything; tell him the whole thing that you are faced with." Frizzell apparently did, and the judge gave the necessary authorization. So once again, a decision had been made and handed down from higher up and then had to be put right with tribal government after the fact. CBS, however, chose not to wait for official clearance. They sneaked into Wounded Knee earlier, and of course the rest of the press got in too.

It was not even eight o'clock when the FBI came to gather up the BIA inventory crew. They were scheduled to go into Wounded Knee tomorrow, May 9, but the FBI was ready to escort them, so they went in this morning instead. I could tell I was close to the end; I had to rest. I went home and lay down, fought it off for several minutes, and then went to sleep. After seventy days, I slept through the reoccupation of Wounded Knee.

I woke up about two hours later and was back in the office by 11:30 A.M. I found that the BIA inventory team had been turned back. It seems that the marshals and the FBI don't communicate with each other any better than they communicate with us. They had gotten their signals crossed, and the marshals were not expecting the inventory team until tomorrow. When the team got to the place of entry, the headmen and chiefs, who were going into the bunkers, as had been agreed, began screaming that the agreement had been violated: no BIA people were supposed to be around; the whole thing was off! Kent Frizzell did what anyone would have done—he turned them back. He wasn't about to lose this hard-fought agreement after all these months.

Jim Legg, a BIA employee who was sent in with the team to photograph the site, was pulled out as well. So Frizzell and Bud Shappard and I went out to Wounded Knee with the express purpose of getting him back to work out there. It took quite a bit of doing, but we got Jim and another fellow, from Land Operations, readmitted. We left them taking their pictures and went to look around. The disorder, the destruction, the wanton disregard for personal property were appalling.

Everywhere were the dirt and debris of weeks of unkempt living: broken and scattered possessions, remains of food, spent cartridges and abandoned weapons, discarded clothing, garbage. Graffiti, signs, and pictures covered the inner walls of the buildings—churches and private homes alike. Some of them were beautiful, like one picture in the basement of the Catholic church of an Indian brave holding aloft a peace pipe. The caption read: "The spirits of my people shall not rest until the forces of man and nature are one, as intended by the Great Spirit. Then and only then will man, nature, and the universe be of one mind." Some were inflammatory or just silly: a swastika, a skull with a long chin and wings, "Death before dishonor, " "U.S.A. stinks!" "Honkies, may your white God forgive you," "Damn, this place looks awful!" "Southern Mescalero AIM," "Gray Mountain was here May 7, 1973," and many others. Some were obscene.

Looking out over the valley, I could see the burned trading post and the museum building, and across to the south, the AIM bunkers, the debris marking the sites of the trailers or tepees, and what was left of the sweat bath. The yellow BIA tractors, blades lowered, dust swirling up behind their tracks, were charging the bunkers and knocking them down. That was a mistake, I think; maybe we should have saved them. I looked again on the cemetery and the monument to those who died in the first Wounded Knee. Now Buddy Lamont is here too, his grave covered with flowers.

I went into the museum. The building itself looked pretty much intact from the outside, but on the inside, what I remember as a beautiful little museum had turned into a pigpen. There was a hole in the floor—I don't know what for. A partition had been added to make two rooms. The relics from the museum were just scattered about like so much junk. There was a pile of probably five hundred arrowheads on the floor, many of them broken, as if they had just been stamped on. Mixed in with them were other artifacts like old pictures, drums, tomahawks, cherry pounders, elk hide scrapers, skulls, headdresses, and the like. All these are Indian artifacts, remembrances of the old Indian way, which is supposed to be prized so highly. I just can't understand it.

Looking around the village, I could see now what had happened to all the material stolen from the construction site. A lot of it was used to set up barricades. The basic design was double walls constructed of plywood nailed onto two-by-eights and packed with dirt in between. Other barricades were reinforced with cinder blocks or sandbags. I saw what appeared to be the AIM headquarters, between the burned-out store and the residence of the Gildersleeves, the owners of the store. A typewriter on a stand and a mimeograph machine marked it as a location of central importance. There were also some old lamps, cigarettes, a tangle of cast-out film from a television camera. Nearby was an old shed with a fresh cowhide thrown over it. Outhouses had been built here and there around the village; now and then a lonesome cat sleeping in an abandoned building or sneaking through the rubble; a puppy lying in the shade by the church.

I went into the Church of God, or what is known as the Little Church. There were quite a few bullet holes visible. There had been a fire started in what appeared to be the altar. The fire had burned part of the piano and part of the walls. Some of the bricks had fallen out, and the ceiling was blackened with smoke. A hole had been cut in the floor on the north side of the church. It had been extended a few feet toward the north and built up with planks, plywood, and cinder blocks into a kind of triangular bunker about eight feet across. There was a slit trench leading from the hole in the floor along the foundation of the church, around the bunker, and out into the open on a slope about twenty feet away.

I also went into the tepee church and into a couple of private homes, one a typical log cabin like the Indians have here on the reservation, the other a house built by the Oglala Sioux Tribe Housing Authority. In all of them, the same dismal picture of destruction, waste, and disregard. Suddenly, in the midst of the nightmare, I realized that there was green grass all around; the grass had gotten green this spring without my noticing it. It was good to see it. Good, too, to see the Ameri-can flag flying properly from the church again, after having seen it flying upside down there during the siege.

Coming back from Wounded Knee, we stopped at the old roadblock 1, which is now the processing roadblock for those coming out of Wounded Knee. There were two buses there, a school bus and a charter bus, waiting to take people back to Pine Ridge. About thirty-five or forty Indians were sitting around in two different groups. A processing line had been set up. The insurgents were, for the most part, easily identifiable. They were different looking folks from the Indians who had manned the citizens' roadblock against them. Their affilia-tion with AIM generally showed in their long hair, feathers, and beads. The FBI agents and marshals were there question-ing these people. Some women marshals were there too, to assist in the search. I don't know how many were arrested or how many residents went back in at this time.

I got back from my trip to Wounded Knee and decided I would go home a little early. On my way out, Jo came run-ning out to the parking lot, calling to me, "Jim Legg has been arrested and is in jail!" I went over to the jail to see what was going on, and by the time I got there, Del Eastman had called Kent Frizzell, and he had arrived just ahead of me. What had happened was that Jim was supposed to accompany some of the FBI agents to do his photographing. He had got separated from his FBI escorts and was just going around on his own, taking pictures everywhere. He is an excellent photographer, by the way, and does a very professional job. One of the mar-shals accosted him, wanted to know what he was doing and, I guess, was a little bit rough about it. Jim smarted off back to him, saying that he was following the instructions of his boss and also of Kent Frizzell, who was, after all, the very top man on the scene. Well, it went from one marshal to another, because Jim was resisting very strongly: he was just doing his job, and he wasn't about to be put out of there a second time. Finally it got to Marshal Wentworth, who was about second in command at the scene, and things became even more heated. Jim, who has quite a temper, blew up and told Wentworth that he was there to take pictures to use as evidence so that the Indians could sue the United States government. That, of course, was very offensive to Marshal Wentworth. He insisted that Jim leave, and Jim said, "If I leave here, you'll have to take me out on my back!" So they put him on his back, handcuffed him, and took him out of there. His teammate from Land Operations was not arrested because, Wentworth said, he did not give them a bad time. By the time I reached the jail Jim was about to be released, but I never saw two more angry individuals than Jim Legg and Marshal Wentworth!

I will close today's entry with some observations by my son, Marty. He was at the jail this afternoon and witnessed some of the processing that was continuing there.

> *Martin Lyman*:
> Wounded Knee is apparently over. This morning Kent Frizzell called to inform my dad that the FBI and the marshals were now occupying Wounded Knee. When they went in, there were over one hundred people still left in Wounded Knee, which is a surprise. This afternoon I saw a crowd of people gathering out in front of the Pine Ridge jail. I wandered over with my camera and sat down. At first it turned out to be mostly people with cameras and a few newsmen. A newsman came over with his mike, his big boom mike, and his portable camera, and they interviewed one of the local supporters of the AIM movement. She was an old woman of about seventy years, short, somewhat withered, dressed in black, but very lively. I found out later that she was Agnes Lamont, mother of the Oglala man killed in Wounded Knee just ten days or so ago.
> Right about then a bus came around the corner, and all of a sudden a crowd began to materialize:

from the street corners, from the steps and lawn of the BIA building, from the filling station. Soon there was a crowd of maybe two hundred people in front of the jail. The bus was carrying militants from Wounded Knee. It was stopping at the jail to pick up several more of the former occupants of Wounded Knee, and then they were all going to Rapid City.

On this particular bus, it was mixed, about half Indian and half white people. There were the typical AIM leaders or individuals who identified with the AIM movement, dressed in blue-jean jackets and cowboy boots, with braided hair and red headbands. The individual on the bus who was the most verbal was a white man of about thirty-five years who was bald and who told someone in the crowd to inform someone else that Baldy was there. He was the one who was doing most of the talking; he knew several people in the crowd, and they apparently knew him. He was speaking out, not viciously, but in a very derogatory yet kind of laughing manner, against the government. The biggest gripe appeared to be in regard to a Bureau of Indian Affairs inventory team which had been sent in this morning, contrary to the terms of the treaty. I learned earlier this morning, when Kent Frizzell called, that these people were accidentally sent in; it was a mistake. Still, it was apparently enough for the militants to grab onto and make an issue of, even though the inventory team was immediately recalled from the field.

As I observed the people on the bus, I tried to make my own guesses as to why they were there. I wondered if the white people were saying, "I have participated in Wounded Knee. I now have another badge to show along with my march in Washington, my march through the South, my associations with Martin Luther King." I wondered whether any of these white people on the bus were able to take a more constructive viewpoint in trying to help the Indians. Or have they just reached their end; have they come to the point where they feel that violence is the only way to solve something? Or are they just here to be on the bandwagon, to be in the limelight, or to raise a little hell?

The crowd surrounding the bus was composed of several different types of people. The nucleus of the crowd was the women who have paraded daily in front of the BIA building, wanting the ouster of Dick Wilson and the superintendent. There was a ring of people around this core group; these were the people who were interested, many of them wavering on whether to be AIM supporters or not. Then, there was a further ring about thirty yards away from the bus; these were people who were not sure of what's going on on either side, people who would rather the whole thing just go away but who were there just out of curiosity.

The marshals had formed a ring around the bus to prevent people from passing anything onto the bus and to keep the crowd back about four or five feet away from the bus. They were taking much abuse from the crowd, but some of them were very, very professional. At the same time, there were other marshals who were not very professional, in my opinion.

All of a sudden Mrs. Lamont, the old woman who was interviewed earlier by the newsman, noticed a man with a camera taking pictures nearby. She yelled out, "He's from the goon squad; he's one of Dick Wilson's goons!" and she charged at him and hit at his camera, trying to knock it to the ground. He was taken somewhat aback, and he looked at her, and laughed, saying, "Why do you do this?" But his laugh was not a genuine laugh; it was one of fear and of being out of place. There was a great tenseness in the crowd. There were shouts from the crowd of "Break his camera!" The man wisely backed off and left. The woman moved back to the center of the crowd in front of the bus and began to cry. The crowd began chanting in support of this woman, and soon the people on the bus joined in the chanting. It continued for maybe five or ten minutes.

The law-enforcement officers finally got everyone out of the jail, and the bus left. There were many cries from the crowd: "Good-bye! Good luck!" "We'll see you in Rapid City!" and that sort of thing. Gradually the crowd dispersed.

As you look at the poverty in Pine Ridge, as you become aware of the prejudice which abounds in this area and the lack of improvement here over the last twenty years, you initially have the reaction that Wounded Knee has been the result, the culmination, of legitimate complaints—which may be true. On further reflection, however, you wonder why some Indians are successful and others are not. Why have some tribes succeeded educationally and economically while others have not? Is it just the personal problems that some Indians have which prevent them from meeting or coping with the challenges of day-to-day life? These are enormous questions and complex ones to which there can be no quick answers, not even from something as drastic as what we have seen at Wounded Knee.

May 9, 1973

I guess you might say that this has been the long fight, this Wounded Knee 1973, and now it is truly over. The village of Wounded Knee has been reoccupied. It is a shambles, a symbol of utter destruction and disorder, created by people who don't care about the things that most of us have been trained to think are important. The long fight not to get anyone killed has been nearly successful. Despite the numbers of wounded, only two have been killed. There may be more; we do not know. But for the public eye, at least, we have lost only two. We could have lost forty!

Now we are preparing to fight another fight, infinitely longer and more difficult: that of putting things together again. We do not even know the material cost of Wounded Knee, and we were arguing about this here in the office today. We do not even have things set up well enough to enable us to determine that cost, but we will do this. The material cost, of course, will certainly be in the millions; but what of the human cost, not even including the two dead and numbers of wounded? The chairman of the tribe and others want now to go back to the situation as it was before, but we can never go back, nor should we. In Wounded Knee, this tribe, this reservation, has gone a long way down the road of discord, and lines have been drawn and hates stated. These lines and this hatred will not be soon erased; they will be with us for a long time to come. I hope that we can now move into the future and somehow build on this experience. As we build with boards and bricks and stones, we can also build with human lives. That is what we must do now, more than ever. A tremendous task, a task that few understand.

May 10, 1973

I went out to Wounded Knee again today, in the company of Wyman Babby. Things were in a little better shape there than they were when I first went in on May 8, the afternoon of the reoccupation. There had been some effort to clean up, to re-organize or carry away. The junk that I saw the other day was not quite so junky. The Catholic church was closed up now, and conspicuously absent was a case of firebombs I had seen earlier on the steps. They were made of quart fruit jars with a wick pushed through the center of the lid. Our Roads people were trying to replace the bridge. I don't know how AIM man-aged it, but the bridge had been burned out, and it collapsed. There was a fairly late-model car in the streambed, and it had been burned, too. It will take about twenty-five thousand dollars to replace that bridge and get the road from Wounded Knee to Porcupine open again. The burned remains of the trading post are perhaps the most visible, and they will be there for a long time.

I had a camera this time, and I got a few pictures. A couple of the FBI agents whom I knew and had worked with took my picture, and I took theirs. The Red Cross was there, feed-ing not the insurgents but the victorious occupation forces. The whole picture was too much like the reoccupation of a war zone, and I suppose that is what it really is. But even war zones can be rebuilt, and so will Wounded Knee. The green grass that I noticed with such satisfaction yesterday will be green for a few weeks longer, and then it will turn brown again, under the sun. Other things will change too, just like the grass; things will improve. A few families have returned already. We got word that the water system has be-come potable, so we're now in business again.

Yesterday the BIA was asked by the White House to help in picking up the pieces of the agreement made by the Department of Justice. It is really the responsibility of the Justice Department, however, and I will very definitely turn it back to them. The role of the BIA will be to stay in the background, to advise, to control a little bit where necessary, to see to it mainly that the constitution of the Oglala Sioux Tribe is upheld. The Justice Department is maintaining quite a presence here still. Kent Frizzell has left for Washington. He called me from the airport in Denver while waiting for his connecting flight. He called not to say good-bye but to tell me that in his absence Wayne Colburn, director of the U.S. Marshal Service, was in charge. This speaks, I think, of a lack of confidence in me personally or in the BIA generally and also of the desire by the Justice Department to maintain control of the situation.

The number of U.S. Marshals on the reservation will be maintained at forty, and there will be a marshal present regularly in Wounded Knee. To Marshal Colburn's credit, he came up with an excellent solution to the problem of our BIA police officers who had had complaints filed against them. As I mentioned before, Frizzell and Colburn had told us to transfer these officers to another location. I had said that I would transfer them only if I was ordered to do so by someone in the direct line of authority of the BIA. Colburn is smooth enough as a politician not to request that kind of order, so what he came up with instead was this: these four individuals will be sent to a thirteen-week training school, put on by the marshals themselves, to train them in all phases of good police work. This idea resolves everything beautifully: it meets AIM's demand that these officers be transferred since, as far as AIM is concerned, they will be away from here for thirteen weeks; it respects my insistence that these officers not be transferred by other than someone in the BIA; and as far as the officers themselves are concerned, they are being trained to make them better policemen rather than just being punished or banished to another duty.

Wyman Babby and I have made one significant step toward the reconstruction effort: we have set up a committee to take control of the reestablishment of Wounded Knee residents.

Wyman and I are a pretty good team; we work together pretty well in achieving some semblance of reasonableness around here. He helped me in selling the concept of the committee to Dick Wilson. At first the chairman couldn't accept it at all, but Wyman presented it to him again in a different way, and he agreed to it on the condition that the reconstruction committee report directly to the executive committee of the tribe. So today we got the committee set up and specified to them whom they will report to. It should work now.

A meeting has been scheduled for May 17 between representatives of the White House and Frank Fools Crow and his followers. The White House people have gotten themselves into a real trap here. Beginning in 1970 or 1971, it became a firm policy in Indian affairs to follow the wishes of elected tribal leadership. The message was clear as it was handed down from the White House, through the Department of the Interior, and, finally, to the level of the various BIA agencies around the country. Now, in order to get a group of militants to lay down their arms at Wounded Knee, the White House has consented to talk meaningfully to a group which represents no one but themselves. These are self-appointed individuals, certainly sincere, who have been crying in the wilderness for many years without being heard. They do not recognize tribal government; these are the ones who want to return to the old Indian ways of a hundred years ago. Indeed, the only way this faction can be satisfied is for the buffalo to return, for the white man to go away, and for the mixed-bloods not to exist. Now the White House is in the position of dealing officially with individuals who are firmly opposed to the system of government for which the White House has proclaimed its support.

Dennis Ickes of the Justice Department's Civil Rights Division is in charge of this meeting, and he has been working pretty hard at getting it all put together. Still, I wonder if the "yellow-tractor syndrome" will once again come into effect. As always happens in Indian business, other people who are sure they know the answers get mixed up in it, and suddenly, when they do not have an answer anymore, they call upon the BIA. I call this the "yellow-tractor syndrome." During this confrontation the BIA has furnished yellow tractors, interpreters, janitors, cars, staff, typewriters, office space, and, of course, advice, which has been seldom heeded. In the case of this meeting, for instance, Dennis Ickes does not want to worry about furnishing food, because that is not his responsibility. Of course he is right, but I have the feeling that Frank Fools Crow will make it Ickes's business by demanding buffalo for food. Ickes is not going to know how to get buffalo, and so he will turn to the BIA. Buffalo, yellow tractors—you see how it is.

More than once in this record, I have expressed my amazement at the extent of knowledge possessed by the FBI. Here is another incident in point: One of the areas of controversy concerning Dick Wilson's administration, as I have said, is his handling of tribal finances. A group of contract auditors and the Justice Department have both been looking into this. Dick told me last night about how thoroughly he was checked out by the FBI. One day a woman from the tribe came to him in his office and told him she needed ten dollars. He was opening the day's mail at the time, and there in one of the envelopes was a five-dollar bill with the explanation, "Use this five dollars however you see fit." So he gave the five dollars to the woman needing money. He said to me, "Do you know that those FBI men even reported that? They knew about even that, and I still don't know how they knew about it."

May 12, 1973

Today is Saturday, and I am on duty here at the office mainly to issue passes into Wounded Knee. This was an idea Moot Nelson had for providing a record of those entering the reoccupied area. In order to be admitted into Wounded Knee, everyone must present a pass from the superintendent's

office. Since this is Moot's project, he, as the assistant superintendent, has been signing most of them; but I will do it
today, and then I will go off duty tomorrow.

We had a little flap over this pass system a couple of days
ago, Thursday, May 10. Three lawyers from the Wounded
Knee Defense Association arrived in Pine Ridge and came
to the office to get their passes. They didn't get the attention they would have liked: they were being held in the BIA
office, they complained, while the FBI search for evidence at
Wounded Knee was continuing, and this was a violation of
the agreement; Kent Frizzell was supposed to have called the
superintendent about this, and the superintendent wouldn't
even talk to them. They seemed to think they were being
most unfairly mistreated.

Jo and Nina are, of course, completely polarized: they
didn't like these anti-establishment lawyers right from the
beginning—two crinkly-haired young men and a hippie-type
young woman—and they liked them less and less the longer
they were there. While I was trying to handle their problem,
they became offensive to Jo and harassed her and ended up
making her really mad. I checked with the two top marshals,
and the word was no entry. Disgruntled, the three went to
the marshals again, and upon persuasion by the lawyers, the
marshals determined that the FBI had by now checked out all
its evidence and so there was no longer any reason to restrict
the lawyers from entering Wounded Knee to represent their
clients. So I issued them the required passes. What I should
have done was make them specify who those clients were. I
forgot this in the hurry of the situation, and it would have
been interesting to know.

I had a good interview today with a reporter from the *New
York Times*. Some interesting points came out relative to
what I was saying the other day about Fools Crow and others
like him. I will include part of the interview here:

> SL: The traditional Indian way of solving differences
> was much different from what we recognize as the

basic principle of majority rule. The adults of the group would get together and talk over the problem, and each one would be heard by the group. Agreement was often obtained, and when it was, this then became the decision of the group. However, if no consensus was reached, then the individuals who did not agree were not bound by the wishes of the majority. In those days, the group disagreeing went over the hill into another river bottom, found their own herd of buffalo, and set up on their own to live according to their own ideas. They could do that in those days, but nowadays, of course, such a thing is not possible.

NYT: Why, do you think, did this traditional system, centered on the chief or headman, change as it did in 1934?

SL: Well, there has been a lot of controversy about that and a lot of opinion expressed in writing. The Indian Reorganization Act of 1934 was, I believe, one of those many laws passed during the Roosevelt administrations. At the time, the country had been in deep depression and was just feeling its way out of it. As I see it, the Indian Reorganization Act was an attempt by John Collier, the commissioner at the time and very much a student of Indian affairs, to strengthen tribal government. It provided the vehicle, more or less on the pattern of the American democracy, by which the federal government could deal with the Indian tribes. Prior to that time the government did not deal with Indian tribes as a body. It had to deal with individuals. The Indian system of selecting leadership did not provide leaders whom the government could deal with in a legal fashion, that is, with regard to agreements, treaties, and things of that kind.

NYT: So the reorganization amounted to an imposition

of American, or Western, values on the traditional Indian way of government?

SL: In a very real sense, yes.

NYT: And this was done, as I understand it, as a measure meant to benefit the Indians?

SL: It did benefit the Indians.

NYT: In what sense?

SL: Since then, the tribes have been exercising the power that was given them under the IRA. They have been constantly growing in tribal strength, and they still are. Tribes throughout the country are very powerful organizations. They have powers similar to a state in that they deal directly with the federal government. And they do govern their own people.

NYT: What were the conditions affecting the Indian tribes back at the time of the Indian Reorganization Act?

SL: The Meriam Report, dating from 1928, describes the Indian situation at that time. The tribes were losing population, for one thing, and they were totally dependent upon the government.

NYT: The government agent under those conditions had a lot of power, then.

SL: He had all the power. He made decisions for individuals and for tribes. Since the IRA, the situation has changed enormously. All decisions relating to tribal business are made, if by the BIA, then only with the consent or concurrence of the Indian tribe. This is contrary to what is popularly believed, that is, that the BIA does all of the business for the Indian.

NYT: Do you think that under the system instituted by the IRA a certain segment of the tribe has been continually left out and discriminated against?

SL: There has been a group left out; they have not been discriminated against, in my opinion. This is the group that wants to go back to the old treaties. They do not recognize the Indian Reorganization Act or tribal government. In the Oglala Sioux Tribe, Frank Fools Crow and Frank Kills Enemy would be two of this group.

NYT: Why do they refuse to go along with the new system?

SL: I think it relates back to the old Indian way: if you do not agree with the majority, you are not bound by the majority decision. At the time of the election of 1935 in which the Oglala Sioux Tribe voted on whether or not to accept the IRA, the vote was very close. There were approximately six thousand people voting, and the issue was carried by a very slim margin: only a few over three thousand voted in favor of the IRA. That left a large segment of the tribe opposed to the changes that were about to come upon them and perhaps not feeling bound by a decision they had not agreed to.

May 14, 1973

Today, Monday, has been a very busy day, one in which we tackled a lot of significant projects. The morning started with the first regular meeting of the reconstruction committee. We got some assignments made for figuring up the costs and for determining who would do the job of the actual reconstruction. We have found that the log houses at Wounded Knee held up better under the occupation and were not damaged to the same extent as the frame-and-wallboard-construction houses of the Pine Ridge Housing Authority. This speaks well for our present thought of rebuilding there with log houses.

Bud Shappard is working on three assignments: a legislative report, a treaty analysis, and a list of the Wounded Knee participants. We want to find out how many of the participants were Oglala Sioux, how many were Indians but not

Oglalas, and how many were non-Indians. We will need to cover about four hundred people altogether; that is about the total number of arrests that were made. Jere Brennan has given me a list of the Wounded Knee residents who stayed there during the siege. They numbered about twenty. He also has listed the families still being housed in the Felix Cohen home and those who are now in trailers. It looks like about thirty-five families are presently being taken care of one way or another. We still have quite a few to go.

We have been speculating the past few days about the status of the council at this time. We have been worried that it could very well be inoperative, and the next election isn't until April of 1974. Those who probably would not come to a council meeting are Jake Little Thunder, Morris Wounded, Birgil Kills Straight, Dick Little, and Hobart Keith. Leo Wilcox, of course, is dead. With those six of the twenty councilmembers not in attendance, that means that the remaining fourteen members must all turn out in order to constitute a quorum. It is by no means certain that this can be accomplished. If just one other member were to be influenced by the five people named, then there would be no quorum and thus no council in session. Bob Ecoffey was saying today that there might be a way: he was thinking in terms of invoking a tribal council resolution which says that in the case of death or resignation of an individual elected to the council, the person who received the next highest number of votes in that election can fill his place. In the case of the absence left by Leo Wilcox's death, this person is Arta Carlow. She is strongly in support of tribal government, and with her as a new councilmember, we could be sure of getting a quorum.

The so-called hit list which was reported to be circulating inside the AIM fortress does indeed exist. Of course, we don't know whether it was, in fact, what you could call a hit list or whether it was just a listing of the "bad guys." Lee Gross, one of our BIA employees, said that he had seen such a list when he was in Wounded Knee the other day surveying the damage. It was a mimeographed sheet and had been placed around in various locations so that everyone could see it. Dick Wilson, Toby Eagle Bull, Stan Lyman, and Wyman Babby were some of the names on the list. I would sure like to see a copy of it for myself.

In contrast to things like that, there are moments of personal satisfaction, like what happened the other day when I saw Matthew High Pine. I knew Matthew twenty years ago as a young, vigorous man. Now he is old and walks with a cane, and I'm sure he doesn't remember me from those old days. Matthew was down in Wounded Knee all during the siege. He came out a few days ago, and when he saw me for the first time he was surprised I was still here. There was a look of genuine delight on his face, and he said, "I am glad you made it!"

May 16, 1973

Preparations have been continuing for the meeting tomorrow between the White House staff and the Fools Crow faction. Frank Fools Crow and his group are taking this meeting very seriously and are really gearing up for it. They have prepared a four-page document to brief the people for the discussions at the hearing. Louis Bad Wound had it duplicated a couple of days ago to distribute to everyone concerned. The Justice Department, too, is anxious that the meeting take place as planned, and, as I've said, Dennis Ickes particularly has been working hard on getting everything arranged.

At the same time, the elected tribal leadership is very unhappy about this meeting. This goes back to the same old conflict between tribal government and the forces of AIM, including the headmen and chiefs, who generally do not have any official position in terms of the elected leadership. As the chairman, the judges, and the executive committee of the Oglala Sioux Tribe see it, why should the White House be meeting with the dissident faction rather than with them, the official tribal leadership, especially when it runs counter to the official, stated federal policy in Indian affairs? All it would take to prevent the Fools Crow meeting from taking place as planned is for the exclusion order barring non-Oglalas from the reservation to be enforced. The tribe, in fact, intended to enforce that order to avoid the risk of any more trouble, since quite a few non-Indians have been filtering in around Kyle over the past few days in anticipation of the meeting. The Department of the Interior is going along with the Department of Justice in supporting the Fools Crow meeting. We have a new man here on temporary assignment from the Interior Department, William ("Bud") Schlick. As senior interior official on the reservation, he has the authority to act with considerable latitude, and he has tackled this situation with determination. He was willing to lay his career on the line in going against what all of us in the BIA have been taught to uphold and forcing a decision not to enforce the exclusion order. After hours of negotiation with the tribal court and the executive committee, it was finally agreed that the court order would be amended in a way that will permit the meeting to take place, although non-Indians will still be kept from the meeting, and roadblocks will be set up to ensure this. It could have led to a real confrontation, but I think we have it headed off now.

The long-standing split between the mixed-bloods and the full-bloods was also evident in another incident these past two days. Yesterday Ellis Chips, one of the traditional headmen and medicine men, like Frank Fools Crow, came to see me in my office. He is an AIM supporter and a believer in the old Indian way. Ellis asked me if I wanted to have a pipe ceremony with him in my office and asked me to bring Dick Wilson, Toby Eagle Bull, and anyone else I would select. I agreed, and the ceremony was set up for today. I asked Dick Wilson if he would come, and he said, "No, I don't want anything to do with that AIM son of a bitch!" Toby Eagle Bull ridiculed the idea that there was anything to this pipe ceremony and mentioned that one of the chiefs who signed the first Wounded Knee agreement had gone home to Wanblee and subsequently went off his rocker completely. He's now in the state hospital at Yankton. I couldn't get anyone else to come either, except Jo Cornelius, who agreed very reluctantly, and Mike Rudy; but I arranged for sandwiches and cookies to be brought in anyway so that it would be nice. Well, Ellis Chips didn't show up today for the ceremony, so we had a bunch of sandwiches and cookies to eat while negotiating on the exclusion order.

Incidentally, when I talked to Dick Wilson yesterday, he told me that he was going to try to get a council together, and he felt confident that he could do this. Also, he had agreed to a meeting with the White House people to be held on the morning of Friday, May 18. So the White House is going to meet with the tribal officials after all. That is something, at least, and it must be a bit of a blow to the Fools Crow faction.

We are still working to total up the cost of the Wounded Knee conflict. I got a telephone call yesterday from Larry Bangs in Senator McGovern's office. He said that the Justice Department has already submitted a bill to the Department of the Interior for five million dollars and that in his estimation the total cost could be well over ten million. He was quite enthusiastic about pushing for money for the reconstruction and such. His plan was to suggest to the senator that the million that we need down here be tacked onto that bill from the Justice Department.

Those enormous figures—one million for this, five million for that, ten million altogether—are indeed impressive, but as a measure of the true cost of Wounded Knee, the human cost in terms of disrupted and even shattered lives, I think we have to look on a much smaller, more personal scale. I took Bud Schlick out to Wounded Knee this afternoon. When we came to the site of the burned trading post, there were Mr. and Mrs. Gildersleeve, the owners of the store. They are an elderly couple, a white man and his Indian wife, who first came to Wounded Knee in 1929. They made their life there, raised some brilliant children, made friends and also, I guess, enemies in the community. They were sitting in the bare yard in front of their burned-out store; they had a few of their belongings around them, which they had gathered up, and they were looking very sad.

They took Bud and me over to their home, which had been used as a hospital during the occupation. It was cleaned up quite a bit from when I saw it that first morning, but it still looked pretty bad. They told us a little of what it was like during the siege. Mrs. Gildersleeve said that there had been wall-to-wall carpet throughout the house, and it was all pulled up, with the exception of that in the bedroom. They didn't know why. The gas furnace ran out of fuel, so the occupiers brought in an old wood stove and mounted it in the bedroom. Extra bunks were built in there too.

Vernon Bellecourt and his wife lived in one room of their house, Mrs. Gildersleeve said; Russell Means lived in a house right next to theirs; and Dennis Banks lived in another a ways down the line. The Gildersleeves were held hostage and were under guard at all times. Their phone was sealed off with tape so that they couldn't dial out. They weren't harmed, she said, but they were very uncomfortable. They had to sleep on the floor with guards surrounding them every night. After the village was first captured, they and other hostages, eleven of them in all, were taken to the Catholic church and held there all evening. They were forced to sit on a narrow board bench against the wall and their feet couldn't touch the floor. They were held there, she said, while their homes were being searched and stripped of anything of value. They lost everything they had, as did everyone else. They watched from the window while their store was looted. Of course it was ransacked before it was burned.

When the senators finally came into Wounded Knee, they cautioned the insurgents about kidnapping charges, and it was at this point, Mrs. Gildersleeve said, that they were released. I wanted to ask her why, when she came out, she said she had not been a hostage; but I didn't feel that I could, under the circumstances. There is a move afoot to reimburse the Gildersleeves through legislation and at the same time to get the tribe to buy the land on which the store was located at fair market value. But even then they will not be compensated; they have lost everything, their entire life's work. There is no way a loss like that can ever be compensated. In seeing them there and talking to them, I could feel that they just could not believe or understand what has happened to them.

Another Wounded Knee victim is George Coats. George is a rancher whose property is just inside the Wounded Knee perimeter. We knew that his place was a major target for the AIM raiders stealing cattle for food, but we didn't quite realize the extent of his losses. I received a letter from him just last Monday. Like the Gildersleeves, his losses, too, are staggering. He told of how "the AIMS," as he called them, would raid his ranch every time there was a cease-fire. The cattle they stole were mainly two- and three-year-old heifers, most of them with calf. They also stole a horse and saddle to herd the cattle with. They killed fifty of his eighty chickens, and the remaining chickens and the pigs could be fed only when George could safely sneak over to the farmyard without being seen.

One night on a raid to his corral, "the AIMS" broke the windows of his house with their rifle butts, fired into the house, and shot at his propane tank. His family waited out the night lying on the floor for safety. After that nightmarish experience, George, his wife and son, and their hired man moved what belongings they could into a small trailer and pulled it the four hundred yards down the road to roadblock 1. After they left, their house was looted and burned to the ground along with most of the corral and seventy-five tons of hay. "The AIMS" actually butchered 63 head of cows, and he lost 125 calves because he couldn't care for the herd properly during the calving season. The man is wiped out. Like he said at the end of the letter, he is a veteran of World War II; he served with distinction in the Pacific and the Philippines. He served his country in its time of need; now who is going to help him out in the face of this disaster, which he did nothing to create?

These are the stories of only two Wounded Knee families.

Multiply their loss and their suffering by that of the dozens of other families, and you begin to glimpse part of the true cost of Wounded Knee 1973.

I met with Bud Schlick and Wyman Babby today and talked to Marvin Franklin on the phone. I didn't really get any satisfaction out of any of them concerning my future as superintendent of Pine Ridge. I guess I'll have to conclude that I've had it here; nobody seems to really think I should stay. At any rate, I'll be going to Tucson at the end of the week to help in the restructuring of the Bureau. While I'm there I'll try to forget about Pine Ridge and have a little fun as well.

June 16, 1973

I have been out of town quite a bit the past month, to Tucson, as I said before, and to Phoenix to get lined up a little better on my job. I took a course there on management by objectives and came away with some fresh perspectives. I got back to Pine Ridge yesterday and spent a couple of hours with Wyman Babby and Bud Schlick in preparation for the hearings that were to take place today and tomorrow, June 16 and 17. Senator Abourezk is conducting the hearings, assisted by Sherman Broadhead from his staff. I was disturbed because Broadhead's attitude at the meeting yesterday was very critical. He was already taking the position that everything we did here at Pine Ridge was wrong: the "goon squads" were running rampant, tribal government had broken down, the agency wasn't active enough or forceful enough in pursuing problems, and a number of things like that.

The first day of hearings was held here at Pine Ridge in Billy Mills Hall. There were about 100 to 150 people present altogether: quite a few full-bloods and many mixed-bloods and, interestingly enough, mostly supporters of Dick Wilson. When Wyman Babby and I arrived at the hearings, Dick Wilson was in the middle of giving his prepared statement, and then he was questioned by the senator. The chairman responded beautifully, composed and sure of himself, as he naturally would be after going through all the things that he had been put to in the past three months. He didn't allow himself to be trapped, which was impressive since the senator was trying to trap people.

Wyman Babby and I were put on to testify right after lunch, at 12:30, and we faced the good senator for three hours. I was a little bit nervous at first, but as time progressed I became less nervous because I found, to my disappointment, that Abourezk did not really want to hear the truth. For instance, he questioned us in great detail about the petition to abolish tribal government, and he simply could not understand the reasons for our actions or the calculations concerning the number of voters. Perhaps he just refused to understand, because I don't think that Wyman or I, either one, have that amount of difficulty getting our points across. In fact, we explained the very same point last night to Sherman Broadhead and he understood it, so I think that Abourezk was just grandstanding for the crowd there in the hall and for the camera crew whom he had brought with him.

It was very disappointing to see the senator today take what appeared to be a purely political position. Anybody can beat the Bureau; it has been a popular sport for many, many years. People of all walks of life, of all persuasions, have stood by and criticized the BIA and in criticizing it have forgotten or been unable to deal with the real issues that relate to Indian people. This is what happened today. Dick Wilson was not a very good target; he is another elected official, like the good senator himself. But Babby and Lyman were good targets, and Abourezk was very unfriendly.

All things considered, I thought we acquitted ourselves pretty well. Still, I was disappointed and disgusted at the shallowness of the senator's questions and the general tone he gave to the sessions. Tomorrow, I am afraid, will be a real donnybrook, judging from the senator's reactions and responses to us today in an atmosphere that was completely friendly toward the Bureau, except for him. Tomorrow, where the witnesses will likely be Russell Means and the Belle-courts and the headmen and chiefs of the reservation—well, I just hate to think of it. They are going to be very vindictive and hostile toward the Bureau, and Abourezk is going to eat it up. So Wyman Babby and Stan Lyman are going to be roasted over a hot fire all day long tomorrow. It's pretty sad that a senator of the United States is willing to approach a situation as explosive as this one by falling into the same old trap of making the Bureau of Indian Affairs a whipping boy, just as it has been down through the years. And of course, this solves no problems.

June 17, 1973

The second day of Senator Abourezk's hearings was held at Kyle. There was some controversy yesterday about the BIA police in Pine Ridge. Someone complained about there being police posted outside Billy Mills Hall and that this was intended to keep them from going in to testify. Abourezk made a big deal about it in the hearing; he called it police-state harassment techniques and insisted that there be no BIA police present anywhere near Kyle for the hearings today. It was really a slap in the face to Del Eastman, and to all of us, in fact. It's going to be pretty difficult to keep up morale in the police force in the face of that kind of action.

We drove out to Kyle in the morning. It was a beautiful day, Father's Day, and with this much rain the countryside was beautiful. The hearings began an hour late, at 11:00 rather than at 10:00. There were about two hundred people there— more than at Pine Ridge yesterday—and they were generally younger.

The people who testified were generally AIM supporters but of varying degrees and types. The first to speak were the headmen Frank Fools Crow, resplendent in all his regalia, and Jim Red Cloud, who spoke through an interpreter. They asked very pointedly for my removal as superintendent of the

Pine Ridge Agency and complained about what they called a breakdown in law and order on the reservation. These traditional elders of the Oglala tribe were followed at the microphone by Russell Means and Ramon Roubideaux. They both testified at length and spoke concerning the demands of AIM and the rationale behind the "New Nation of Oglala," that is, why it was necessary, in their minds, to take over Wounded Knee. Wyman Babby and I were on hand and spoke when we were asked to provide information, to account for our actions in a certain regard, or to respond to specific accusations. Sharing the microphone with Means and Roubideaux is an experience I won't forget.

Abourezk had said earlier, in response to the testimony of Fools Crow and Red Cloud, "You and the other witnesses are here to tell us what is wrong with the BIA. Even if I removed this superintendent, which I do not have the power to do, another one will take his place, and things will not necessarily change. It may be the policy, not the people, that is wrong." Following that line, a long string of Pine Ridge residents, plus a couple of neighboring Yankton Sioux and Rosebud Sioux, proceeded to tell him. Included were many of the people who were active in AIM and in the impeachment attempt against Dick Wilson or whose names have otherwise figured prominently in this narrative: Gerald One Feather, Charles Under Baggage, Vern Long, Dave Long, Delores Swift Bird, Louis Bad Wound, Hildegard Catches, and Birgil Kills Straight. They spoke both about general concerns and about specific grievances regarding the treatment of individuals. Ethel Merrival wanted to speak, but it was pretty late. She only wanted five minutes, but Abourezk said, "We have got to close. I have let too many people talk too much already." The meeting concluded with a beautiful rendition of the Sioux national anthem, and we all left.

As I walked out, the dominant thought in my mind was that I had just spent a Saturday and a Sunday listening to things that were not very productive. I would have gladly given these two days, and all the rest of the time I have spent working to resolve the Wounded Knee conflict, working instead at almost any kind of thing that would have made the Oglala situation better. I do resent having been forced to expend my time and my skill this weekend, as well as during all the weeks and months of the AIM intrusion, on something that is essentially negative. And the losers in all of this, God bless them, are the Oglalas.

July 13, 1973

On my way to Rapid City a couple of days ago, I drove through Wounded Knee. The land was beautiful: rolling hills, rich grass, here and there a draw filled with trees, Porcupine Butte in the background. As you come over Wounded Knee Hill, you get the first glimpse of the pastoral-looking village of Wounded Knee, now a symbol of hate, frustration, and failure. The white Catholic church is gone from the hill where it once stood as a landmark. Always before, the church identified the community; now, as you approach, you must identify the community first and then you realize that the church is not there anymore. Only the concrete remains of its foundation are silhouetted against the sky.

Reconstruction in Wounded Knee is progressing pretty well. In the town of Pine Ridge things are nearly back to normal. The BIA building has been repainted, and there are no visible scars. There is still a bullet hole in the ceiling, but no one will notice it. People are beginning to come back in; the BIA building is once again at the service of everyday Indian business. I have often thought in retrospect that it was a grave error for the command post and headquarters of the war operation to be located in our BIA building. It just drove the people away. Chairman Dick Wilson got a quorum the last time he called a meeting of the council. The chairman and the council went into a two-week session on July 10, so it looks like tribal government is back in business as well.

Yesterday, July 12, the Oglala Sioux Tribal Council, with fifteen members present, one more than the fourteen needed to make a quorum, voted unanimously to keep me at Pine Ridge. This now puts me in a quandary. I am all committed to go to Phoenix, where I would be working in the new Trust Protection Unit of the area office there. I have been working at it already, and, in fact, I have made a good start in getting that office set up down there. Besides, June and I have wanted to go to Phoenix for a long time. I talked to the boss, Marvin Franklin, this morning, and he wants me to stay, too. I told him that I could not change directions like that from one hour to the next and that I would have to consider it. Right now I think I will tell Assistant Secretary Franklin that my preference is to go to Phoenix but that if he wants me to stay in Pine Ridge I will do it.

Epilogue

Stanley Lyman did stay on temporarily as superintendent of the Pine Ridge Indian Reservation until November of 1973. It was during this frustrating and indecisive time that Stan was informed that he would be "slowly" and "quietly" transferred to the Phoenix Area Office of the BIA. His remaining three years with the Bureau of Indian Affairs were spent working to protect Indian land, water, and resource rights as head of the new Trust Protection Unit in Phoenix. He retired in 1976 because of ill health.

It would be tempting to say that the above narrative represents some epic turning point in the history of Indian affairs in the United States. Such is not so. Sixteen years after the affair was over and after many of the players were gone, life goes on at Pine Ridge in much the same fashion as it did before Wounded Knee 1973. It has been exceedingly difficult to attract industry and private enterprise to the Sioux area since the upheaval. While it might also be tempting to call some people heroes and others villains, that is likewise not within the realm of reason. As Stan Lyman later remarked, "Damn it, there are no winners!"

Our narrator died on January 21, 1979, of congestive heart failure. June Kremer Lyman continues to live an active life in Phoenix, Arizona.

Additional Reading

It is surprising that an incident such as Wounded Knee II, which created such a national and international stir, could have produced so few books, particularly when one considers the drama, the conflict, and the people in high places who were involved. Wounded Knee II was in part a struggle between the various divisions of the federal government and other segments of the white community, but it was also a struggle between divisions of American Indians. There is no one volume to which one can refer as the single authoritative work on the subject of Wounded Knee II. What has emerged instead is a series of partial (and partisan) reports.

The following is a short bibliography of materials that will contribute something to the understanding of the overall picture. Lyman's narrative itself is important to this understanding because of its immediacy, and it is hoped that future writers will profit from this eyewitness account.

Akwesasne Notes staff, comps. and eds. *Voices from Wounded Knee*. Rooseveltown, N.Y.: *Akwesasne Notes*, n.d.

Boly, Peter. "Ethnic Identity and Cultural Resistance: Oglala-Sioux of the Pine Ridge Reservaton Today." In *North American Indian Studies 2; European Contributions, Society and Art*, edited by Peter Hovens, 204–24. Gottingen: Edition Herodot, 1984.

Burnett, Robert, and John Koster. *The Road to Wounded Knee*. New York: Bantam, 1974.

Brand, Joanna. *The Life and Death of Annie Mae Aquash*. Toronto: Lorimer, 1978.

Collier, Peter. "Wounded Knee: The New Indian War." *Ramparts* 11 (January 1973): 25–29, 56–59.

Collins, Paul. "Showdown at Wounded Knee: Black Artist Sketches Indian Confrontation." *Ebony* 28 (June 1973): 46–48, 50, 52–54, 56.

Deloria, Vine, Jr. *Behind the Trail of Broken Treaties*. Dell, 1974. Reprint. Austin: University of Texas Press, 1985.

Dewing, Rollard. "South Dakota Newspaper Coverage of the 1973

Occupation of Wounded Knee." *South Dakota History* 12, no. 1 (1982): 48–64.

———. *Wounded Knee: The Meaning and Significance of the Second Incident.* New York: Irvington Publishers, 1985.

Dilley, Russell. "NCC's Role at Wounded Knee." *Christian Century* 90 (April 4, 1974): 400–402.

———. "Standoff at Wounded Knee." *Christian Century* 90 (May 9, 1973): 527–28.

Dollar, Clyde. "The Second Tragedy at Wounded Knee: A 1970s Confrontation and Its Historical Roots." *The American West* 10 (September 1973): 4–11.

Doyle, Barrie. "Bury My Tithe at Wounded Knee." *Christianity Today* 17 (June 8, 1973): 40–41.

Eicher, Carl K. "Constraints on Economic Progress on the Rosebud Sioux Indian Reservation." Ph.D. diss., Harvard University, 1960.

Elbert, Ted. "Wounded Knee: A Struggle for Self-Determination." *Christian Century* 90 (March 28, 1973): 356–57.

Fishlow, David. "Reading the Riot Act." *New Republic* 169 (July 21, 1973): 11–12. (Concerning the arrests after Wounded Knee.)

Hanlon, Susan L. M. "Renegades: The Second Battle of Wounded Knee." *American Opinion* 16 (May, 1973): 1–14.

Johansen, Bruce. "Leonard Peltier and the Possee: Still Fighting the Indian Wars." *Nation* 225 (October 1, 1977): 304–7.

Josephy, Alvin M., Jr., *Now That the Buffalo's Gone.* New York: Knopf, 1982.

———. "Wounded Knee and All That—What the Indians Want." *New York Times Magazine* (March 18, 1973): 18–ff.

Lyman, Stanley D. Papers, 1923–79.

Matthiessen, Peter. *Indian Country.* New York: Viking Press, 1984.

———. *In the Spirit of Crazy Horse.* New York: Viking Press, 1983.

Messerschmidt, Jim. *The Trial of Leonard Peltier.* Raritan, N.J.: South End Press, 1984.

Ortiz, Roxanne Dunbar. *The Great Sioux Nation: Sitting in Judgment on America.* American Indian Treaty Council Information Center/Moon Books, 1977. (Based on and containing testimony heard at the Sioux Treaty Hearing held December 1974 in federal district court, Lincoln, Nebraska.)

———. *Indians of the Americas: Human Rights and Self-Determination.* New York: Praeger Publishers, 1984.

Powers, Marla. *Oglala Women.* Chicago: University of Chicago, 1986.

Proto, Brian L. "The Policy Process in American Indian Affairs: Patterns of Interaction between American Indian Interest Groups, the BIA, and the Indian Affairs Committees of the Congress." Ph.D. diss., Miami University, 1979. (On the decline of AIM and the 1967–77 rise of NCAI and NTCA.)

Ranck, Lee. "Siege at Wounded Knee." Engage/Social Action 1 (May 1973): 6–21.

Roos, Philip D., Dowell H. Smith, Stephen Langley, and James McDonald. "The Impact of the American Indian Movement on the Pine Ridge Indian Reservation." Phylon 41, no. 1 (1980): 89–99.

Schultz, Terri. "Bamboozle Me Not at Wounded Knee." Harper's 246 (June 1973): 46–48, 53–56.

Talbert, Carol. "Experiences at Wounded Knee." Human Organization 33 (Summer 1974): 215–17.

Taylor, Theodore. "The Trail of Broken Treaties, Wounded Knee, and the Longest Walk." In American Indian Policy. (Lomond: Mount Airy, Md., 1983), 34–44.

Tilsen, Kenneth E. "U.S. Courts and Native Americans at Wounded Knee." Guild Practitioner 31 (Spring 1974): 61–69.

U.S. American Indian Policy Review Commission, Task Force 2. "Bureau of Indian Affairs' Support for the Functions of Tribal Government—Case Study of Pine Ridge Reservation." Tribal Government (1976), Appendix 16, 335–55.

U.S. Congress. Senate. Committee on Interior and Insular Affairs. Subcommittee on Indian Affaris. Occupation of Wounded Knee: Hearings before the Subcommittee on Indian Affairs. 93d Cong., 1st sess.; June 16, 1973, Pine Ridge, South Dakota; June 17, 1973, Kyle, South Dakota.

U.S. Court of Claims. The Innocent Victims of the Occupation of Wounded Knee, South Dakota v. the United States. Defendant's Pretrial Submission on Liability, December 3, 1979. Defendant's Requested Findings of Fact and Brief to the Trial Commissioner, February 1981.

Wall, James M. "Wounded Knee Comes to Trial." Christian Century 91 (March 6, 1974): 251–52.

Weyler, Rex. Blood on the Land: The Government and Corporate War against the American Indian Movement. New York: Everest House, 1982.

Zimmerman, Bill. Airlift to Wounded Knee. Chicago: Swallow Press, 1976.

Index